"B" Is for Bugs

by Annalisa McMorrow
illustrated by Marilynn G. Barr

Publisher: Roberta Suid
Design & Production: Standing Watch Productions
Cover Design: Susana Siew-Demunck

Originally published by

Republished in Australia by

HAWKER BROWNLOW
E D U C A T I O N

P.O. Box 580, Cheltenham,
Victoria 3192, Australia
Phone: (03) 9555 1344 Fax: (03) 9553 4538
Toll Free Ph: 1800 33 4603 Fax: 1800 15 0445
Website: http://www.hbe.com.au
Email: brown@hbe.com.au

©2001 Monday Morning Books, Inc
©2003 Hawker Brownlow Education

Printed in Australia

ISBN: 1 74025 897 5
Code: #MMA-2124

Contents

Introduction   4
Insect & Spider Facts   6
Buggy Portfolio   7

Week One:
LANGUAGE: Insectlopedia   9
MATHS: Ant Farm Maths   11
SCIENCE: I'm an Insect   13
SPELLING: Bed Bug Bulletin Board   14
ART: Beautiful Beetle Books   17
GAME: Bug on Your Back   18
SONGS: Aphid Songs   20
TAKE HOME: Bug Tallies   21

Week Two:
LANGUAGE: "Why" Stories   23
MATHS: Buggy Graph   24
SCIENCE: Very Bad Bugs   25
SPELLING: Lightning Bug Spelling   27
ART: Beaded Bees   30
GAME: Pin the Spot on the Ladybird   31
SONGS: Bee Song   32
TAKE HOME: Insect Concentration   33

Week Three:
LANGUAGE: Mary Had a Little Bug   35
MATHS: Ladybird Lessons   37
SCIENCE: Insect Stages   38
SPELLING: Butterfly Behaviour   40
ART: Mâché Metamorphosis   43
GAME: Who Wants to
         Be an Entomologist?   44
SONGS: Butterfly Song   46
TAKE HOME: Insect Camouflage   47

Week Four:
LANGUAGE: Calming Miss Muffet   49
MATHS: Super Spider Maths   50
SCIENCE: Eight-Legged Reports   52
SPELLING: Web of Words   54
ART: Web Weaving   57
GAME: Wheel of Wonder   58
SONGS: Spider Songs   60
TAKE HOME: Spotting Spiders   61

Insect Book Links   63
Insect Diploma   64

Introduction

B Is for Bugs is a month-long unit that introduces children to the world of insects through informative and exciting cross-curriculum activities. Bug-related language, maths, science, art, song, spelling, homework, and game activities are featured for each week.

Use the "Bug Facts" and "Spider Facts" (p. 6) to introduce the unit. This sheet explains the characteristics of bugs and spiders. Point to the differences between true insects and spiders. Then help children make their Buggy Portfolios. They can use these to store all of their bug-related business in the classroom or to take materials home.

Patterns throughout the unit can serve many purposes. For instance, duplicate the patterns from the "Bug on Your Back" game for use as name tags, or desk labels, or enlarge them to use as bulletin board decorations.

The activities in *B Is for Bugs* are intended for students in year one to year three. Some lessons may easily be simplified for younger children. For instance, if children cannot write their own reports or stories, they can dictate them to the teacher or teacher's helper.

Graphic organisers accompany two activities. These forms help the children to stay focused on the topics that they are researching or learning about.

Throughout the unit, "Did You Know…" facts appear on the teacher resource pages. Share these facts with the children, then have them look for facts on their own to share with their classmates.

The unit ends with a final game that allows children to share the knowledge that they've learned over the four weeks of study. Once children have finished the game, give the students Insect Diplomas (p. 64), to show that they have mastered the world of bugs.

To extend the *B Is for Bugs* unit, look for bug-related books to store in your reading corner. (Several activities include book links about featured bugs.) Children can spend free time learning more about the insects they're studying. Note that some books have an easy tie-in, such as the spider in *Charlotte's Web*. Challenge children to be on the lookout for mentions of insects in the books and magazines that they read on their own.

Also be on the lookout for games, puzzles, and toys with an insect or spider theme. Some popular books, such as *Miss Spider's Tea Party*, have game tie-ins.

If possible, invite an entomologist to visit the classroom and discuss bugs.

The Web is a good place to locate information about insects and spiders to share with the students. Older children may be able to surf the Web themselves. Younger children may need assistance. Several websites are listed below as a staring point. Remember, websites change with frequency. Always check the sites yourself before sharing them with the students.

Bug Sites:

Bugbios
http://www.insects.org

Yahoo Insect Directory Listings
http://dir.yahoo.com/Science/Biology/Zoology/Animals
__Insects__and_Pets/Insects/

The Bug Club is an introduction to entomology (bug science)
http://www.ex.ac.uk/bugclub/

School Community Environment Program
http://www.arandaps.act.edu.au/environment/activity/
humus/beasties/buglinks.htm

Insect & Spider Facts

Bug Facts

Insects have three different body parts: the head, the thorax, and the abdomen. They have a hard covering on the outside of their bodies. This is an external skeleton. It is called an exoskeleton. The exoskeleton encases their organs and protects them in the manner of a suit of armour.

Insects have three pairs of legs. These six legs are attached to the middle part of their body, which is the thorax. Although many insects have wings, some insects, such as most ants, do not have wings. Insects also have antennae.

Insects can be found in different environments. Some live on dry land, while others live in or near water. Most insects eat by sucking plant juices. However, some suck the blood of other insects and spiders. Others feed on humans and other animals.

Insects include ants, aphids, bees, beetles, butterflies, cockroaches, flies, grasshoppers, mosquitoes, moths, and wasps. Many people confuse other creatures with insects. For example, centipedes, millipedes, and spiders are not insects.

Spider Facts

Spiders are arachnids. Other arachnids include scorpions, ticks, and mites. Spiders have two body parts and four pairs of jointed legs. Spiders also have a pair of mouth parts that end with fangs. Unlike insects, arachnids do not have antennae.

A spider's eyes, legs, and jaws are on the front of its body. The back part of a spider's body, which is much larger than the front part, has a set of little taps called spinnerets. The spider uses these to spin its web.

Spiders spin webs in order to catch insects. The web traps the insect, which the spider then eats. A web is sticky and makes it difficult for an insect to escape. A spider also lives on its web. The spider knows which threads are sticky and which aren't. It only walks on the threads that are not sticky.

Not all spiders spin webs. Flower spiders hide near flowers. Jumping spiders find insects in the grass and trees. Trapdoor spiders make a nest underground. Then they jump out and catch insects!

Buggy Portfolio

Materials:
Portfolio Patterns (p. 8), scissors, crayons or textas, glue, hole punch, wool, legal-sized folders or large sheets of heavy paper

Preparation:
Photocopy a copy of the Portfolio Patterns for each child.

Directions:
1. Portfolios can be made in a variety of ways. Demonstrate at least one way for the children. If using legal-sized folders, punch holes along the two open sides. Cut two arm-length pieces of wool and tie knots in one end of each. Thread the wool through the holes and tie the free ends together to make a strap. If using paper, fold the paper in half to make a folder, and then continue as described above. If making portfolios as shown in the picture, punch two holes on opposite sides, thread through with a piece of wool, and tie. Consider sealing the sides with tape or staples.
2. Give each child a sheet of patterns to colour and cut out.
3. Have the children decorate their portfolios with the patterns.

Options:
• The children can add their own hand-drawn insect or spider pictures, as well. Or they can cut out pictures from magazines to glue to their portfolios.
• Cover the portfolios with contact paper for added sturdiness. Reinforce the holes with hole reinforcers.

Portfolio Patterns

Insectlopedia

This activity introduces children to research by having them make their own miniature insect encyclopedias. Graphic organisers help them stay focused.

Materials:
Insectlopedia Graphic Organiser (p. 10), encyclopedias, paper, pens or pencils

Preparation:
1. Photocopy a copy of the Insectlopedia Graphic Organiser for each child.
2. Gather encyclopedias for children to use.

Directions:
1. Give each child a graphic organiser.
2. Explain that the children will be using encyclopedias to gather information about insects.
3. Have the children fill out the graphic organiser, then use the encyclopedia to gather information.
4. The children can transfer their information to sheets of writing paper, making their own encyclopedia-like entries.
5. Have the children add to their "insectlopedias" throughout the month. They can also share their facts with friends and family.

Options:
• Have the children use construction paper to make covers for their insectlopedias. Use paper fasteners to bind their pages into the covers.
• Younger children can dictate their questions and draw pictures of the insects they're researching.

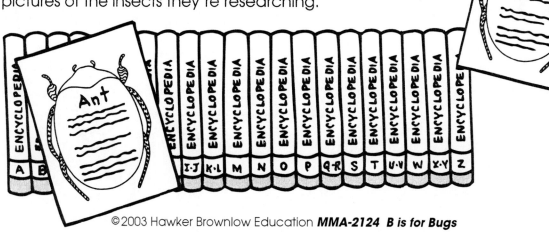

Insectlopedia Graphic Organiser

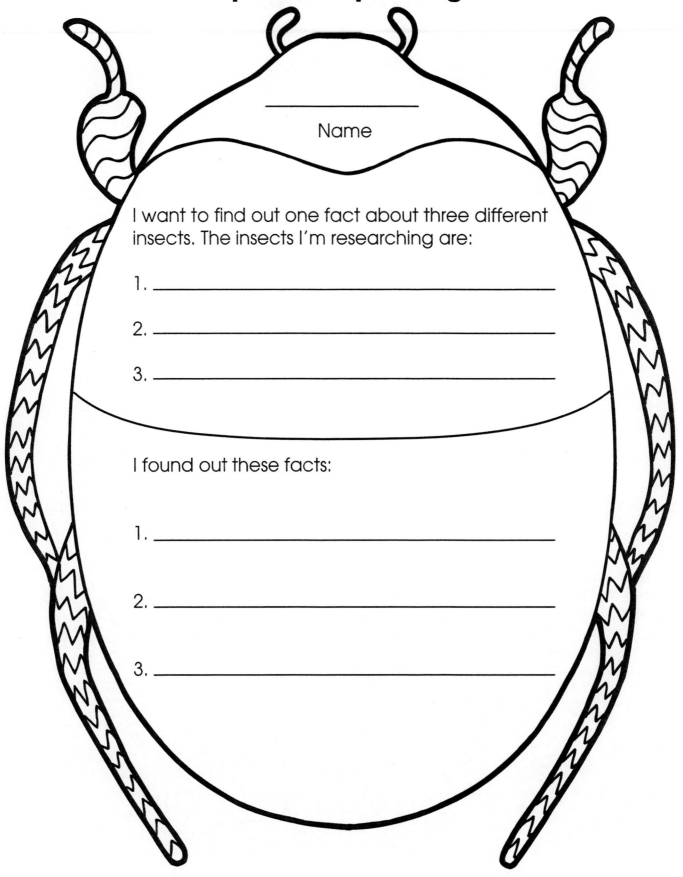

_____
Name

I want to find out one fact about three different insects. The insects I'm researching are:

1. _____

2. _____

3. _____

I found out these facts:

1. _____

2. _____

3. _____

Ant Farm Maths

This activity can be used for different levels of mathematical study. For younger children, write a plus or minus sign in the middle ant of each equation. Write in a multiplication sign for older children.

Materials:
Ant Farm (p. 12), pencils, crayons or textas

Preparation:
1. Fill in the missing signs (+, -, or x), then duplicate the Ant Farms. Make one for each child.
2. Make an answer key for self-checking, if desired.

Directions:
1. Give each child a copy of the Ant Farm.
2. Have the children do the problems and then share their answers with the class. Or they can use the answer key for self-checking.

Options:
• For older children, pass out the Ant Farms without any signs written in the middle ants. Let the children make their own problems. They can add a +, -, or x and then write the answers on the back. Have the children trade papers.
• To make the problems more difficult, white-out the numbers on the ants and write in your own numerals.

Did You Know...
An ant nest has many rooms. The rooms are connected with tunnels. Each nest has a queen and many worker ants.

Ant Farm

I'm an Insect

Materials:
Paper, pencils, crayons or textas

Preparation:
None

Directions:
1. Discuss the characteristics of all insects: they have three body parts and six legs. Insects include beetles, moths and butterflies, wasps, ants, bees, flies, mosquitoes, and grasshoppers. Spiders are not insects.
2. Have each child choose one insect characteristic that he or she might like to have. Or children can choose which insect they would like to be.
3. Give each child a sheet of paper and a pencil. Have the children write a short story (about one paragraph long) describing what it would be like to have the chosen characteristic or be the specific insect. For example, a child might write about wanting wings in order to fly.
4. Children can illustrate their papers.

Option:
• Have the children write papers called "I'm Not an Insect". For this assignment, they choose one feature and say why they are glad not to have it.

Note:
• Younger children can dictate their stories.

Bed Bug Bulletin Board

Materials:
Bed Bugs (p. 15), Bed (p. 16), bag, construction paper, scissors, coloured textas

Preparation:
1. Photocopy a copy of the Bed Bugs for each child and one for teacher use.
2. Cut the bugs apart and colour as desired.
3. Enlarge the Bed pattern and post on a bulletin board.

Directions:
1. Announce a date for a spelling "bee".
2. Divide the students into small groups. Have the children work together to learn the words. Let the children take the Bed Bugs home to study.
3. On the day of the spelling bee, put the bugs in a bag. Pull one bug from the bag at a time and have a child from each group spell the word on the bug.
4. If the child spells the word correctly, he or she can stick the bug on the bed. If not, another child from that group tries to spell the word.
5. Continue until each child has a chance to spell one word and all of the bugs are stuck on the board.

Options:
• Write additional spelling words in the blank bugs.
• If the words are too difficult, white-out the given spelling words and write in your own. (Simple insect-related word lists might include ant, bee, bug, wing, egg.) Photocopy these for the class.
• Use the words on the list for a match-up activity. Have the children match the two words that are related. The answers are bee/hive, butterfly/cocoon, ladybird/beetle, larvae/mosquito.

Bed Bugs

Bee

Beetle

Butterfly

Cocoon

Hive

Ladybird

Larvae

Mosquito

Bed

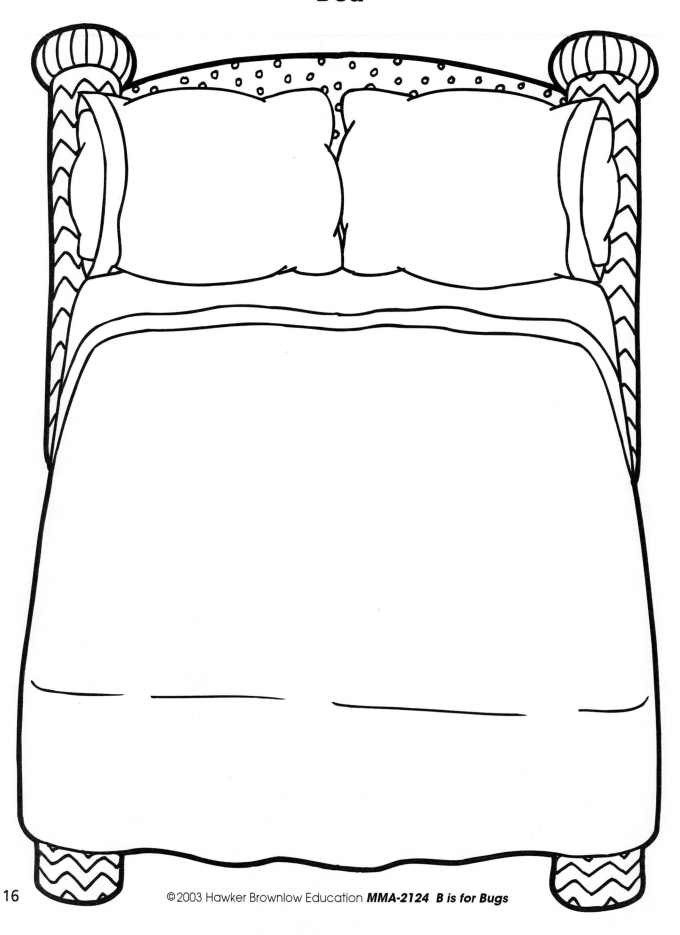

Beautiful Beetle Books

Most scientists keep journals to record observations about experiments. Treat your students like real scientists and have them keep their own bug books. They can draw pictures of bugs that they see outside of the classroom in their books.

Materials:
Coloured paper, crayons or textas, drawing paper, scissors, hole punch, wool or paper fasteners

Preparation:
None

Directions:
1. Explain that beetles have hard, opaque, waterproof wings that cover their thinner flight wings. These wings look like a shell. (Children may have seen the hard, outer wings of a ladybird.)
2. Discuss the fact that some beetles are brightly coloured and patterned. If possible, show pictures from a book.
3. Let the children choose coloured paper to use for their book covers. They should cut the paper into oval shapes—one for the front cover and one for the back.
4. Have the children cut white drawing paper into ovals that are the same size as the book covers. They can add designs to the covers using crayons or textas.
5. Help the children bind their books with wool or paper fasteners.
6. The children can use the books to keep track of bugs they see during the unit.

Note:
• Provide ovals cut from cardboard for children to trace, if desired.

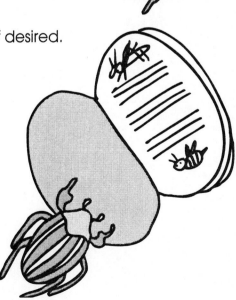

Bug on Your Back

Materials:
Bugs (p. 19), scissors, tape

Preparation:
1. Photocopy enough bug patterns so that each child can have one. More than one child can have the same pattern.
2. Cut the patterns apart.

Directions:
1. Tape one pattern to each child's back. (Don't let the children see their own patterns.)
2. Have the children walk around the room and talk to each other. During their conversations, they will try to give subtle clues to each other as to which bug they're wearing. For example, one child might say, "I'm glad I spotted you," to a child wearing a ladybird. Or a child might say, "Why don't you hop over to talk to me," to a child with a grasshopper pattern. Once the children have correctly guessed their bug, they can sit down or help others with clues.

Options:
• Let children draw pictures of bugs. Cut these out and use them as the patterns for the game.
• Help children to develop different clues ahead of time.
• Choose only patterns that children are familiar with.

Did You Know...
A bee's stinger only comes out when it's ready to sting. Other times, the stinger is in its stomach!

Bugs

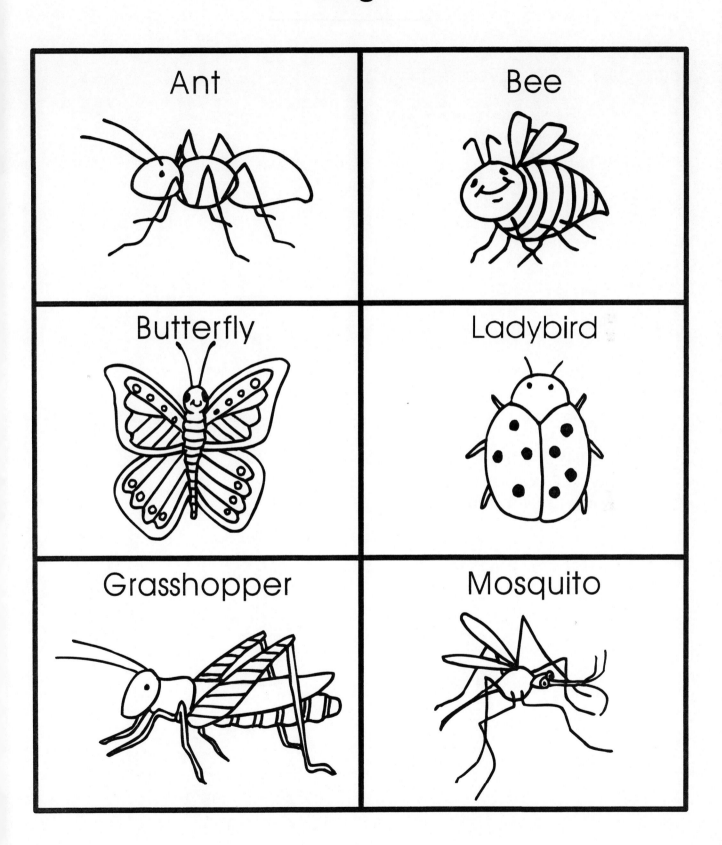

Ant

Bee

Butterfly

Ladybird

Grasshopper

Mosquito

Aphid Songs

Aphids on Roses
(to the tune of "My Favourite Things")

Aphids on roses and fleas on my kittens
Cockroaches munching.
Mosquitoes! I'm bitten!
Bright yellow jackets that zoom through the air
Landing on people without any care.

When a bug bites,
When a bee stings,
When a wasp gets mad,
I simply look at all the good things bugs bring,
And then I don't feel so bad.

They'll Be Eating All the Roses
(to the tune of "She'll Be Coming
        'round the Mountain")

They'll be eating all the roses when they come.
        When they come!
They'll be eating all the roses when they come.
        When they come!
They'll be eating all the roses,
They'll be eating all the roses,
They'll be eating all the roses,
        When they come!

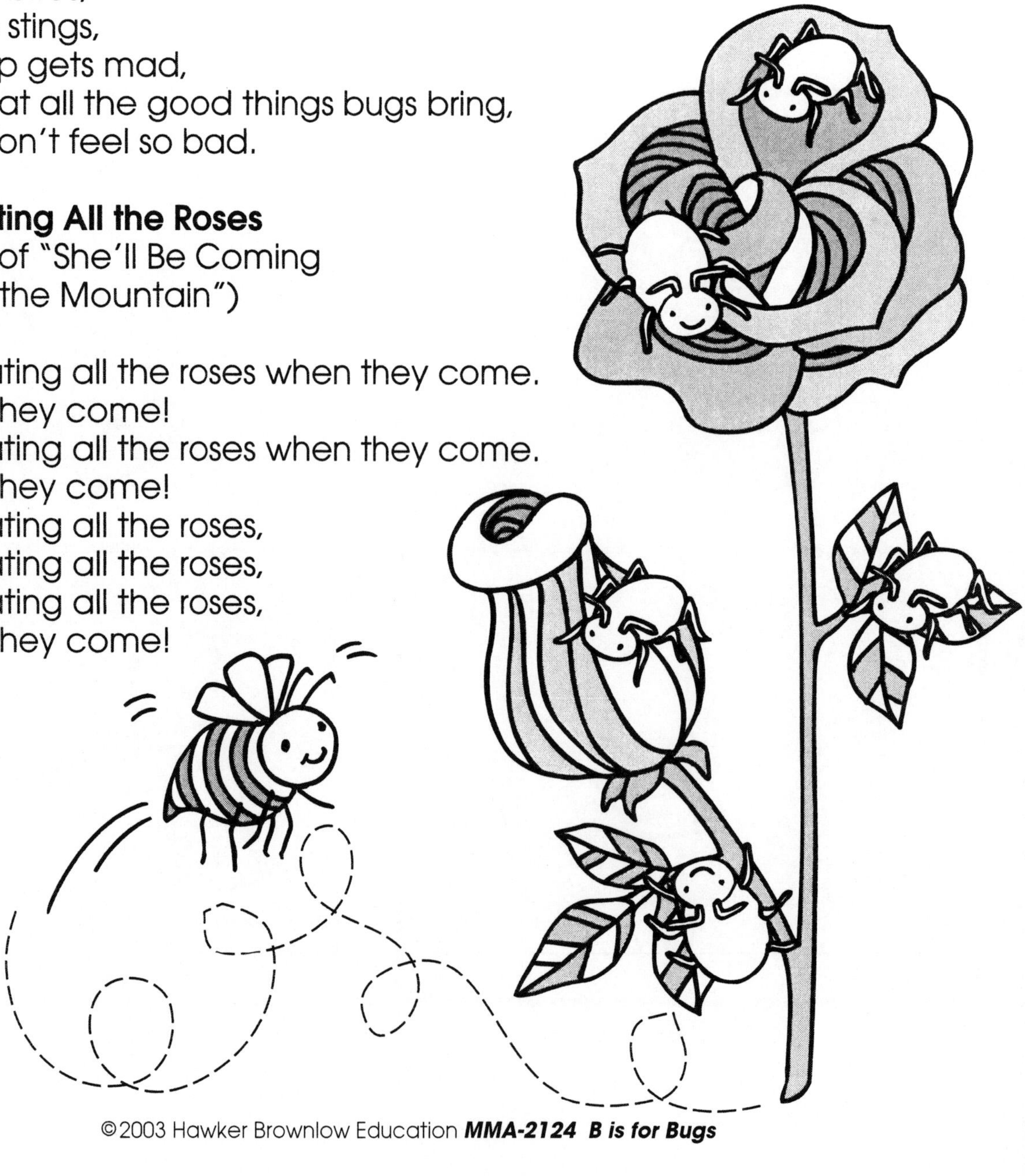

Bug Tallies

Materials:
Bug Tally (p. 22), paper, pencils

Preparation:
Photocopy a copy of the Bug Tally for each child.

Directions:
1. Give each child a Bug Tally to take home. Explain that the children are to make marks for each of the bugs that they see in one afternoon and evening. (If they see many of one bug—such as an ant—they can stop at ten.)
2. If children see bugs that aren't on the tally, they can turn the paper over and draw the bugs on the back.
3. Remind the children not to disturb the bugs and to avoid any that might sting them!
4. Have the children bring their tally sheets back to share with the class.
5. Save the sheets for the Buggy Graph activity (p. 24).

Option:
• If the children see bugs that they cannot readily identify, use bug resources to find the names of the mystery insects.

Did You Know...
Even young fireflies glow. The eggs, larva, and chrysalis all shine!

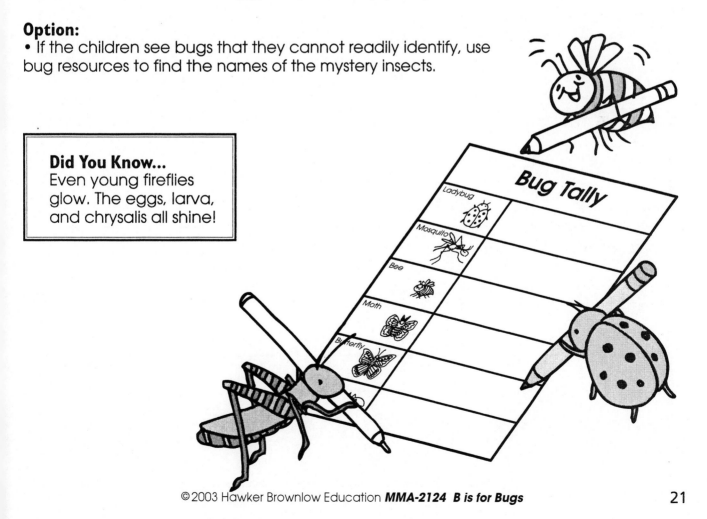

Bug Tally

Ladybird	
Mosquito	
Bee	
Moth	
Butterfly	
Ant	

"Why" Stories

Materials:
Why Mosquitoes Buzz in People's Ears: A West African Tale by Verna Aardema (Scholastic, 1980), chalkboard and chalk or large paper and textas, paper, pencils, crayons or textas, hole punch and paper fasteners (for binding book)

Preparation:
None

Bee	Buzzes
Grasshopper	Hops
Ladybird	Flies
Firefly	Lights up

Directions:
1. Read the children the book *Why Mosquitoes Buzz in People's Ears.*
2. Discuss how this story gives an explanation of why an insect does a specific thing.
3. Have the children name traits of different insects. Make a list on the chalkboard or on a sheet of paper. In one column, write names of insects. In a second column, write their traits. (You can write down more than one trait per insect. For instance, next to "bee" you might have "buzzes", "flies around", and "makes honey".)
4. Give each child a sheet of paper and a pencil. Have the children write their own "why" story about how an insect got its trait. For instance, they might write about why crickets chirp, fireflies light up, or grasshoppers hop. They can choose from the list, or they can brainstorm their own insects.
5. Have the children illustrate their stories.
6. Either hang the "Why" stories on a bulletin board, or bind them together in a classroom insect book.

Note:
• Younger children can dictate their stories or draw pictures as explanations of the traits.

Buggy Graph

Children will use the information from their Bug Tallies to make a classroom graph.

Materials:
Bug Tallies (p. 21), Bug Tally (p. 22), large sheet of paper, scissors, drawing paper, sticky tape, crayons or textas

Preparation:
1. Enlarge and photocopy the bugs from the bug tally and cut them out.
2. Make a bar graph on the large sheet of paper. At the top of each column, tape one of the bugs. Leave several blank columns at the end. Each square should equal five insects.

Directions:
1. Work with the children to fill out the graph. Tally the amount of each type of bug the children saw. If the children found bugs that are not given as patterns, then have them draw the bugs and add them to the blank columns.
2. Help the children read the finished graph.
3. Hang the graph in the classroom near the books about bugs.

Option:
• Make graphs for bugs that the children see at school. Each time .the children spot a bug, they can add it to the graph.

©2003 Hawker Brownlow Education *MMA-2124 B is for Bugs*

Very Bad Bugs

In this activity, the children will write about harmful bugs as if they were enemies in a comic strip.

Materials:
Bad Bugs Organiser (p. 26), pens or pencils, drawing paper, crayons or textas, encyclopedias or books about bugs

Preparation:
Photocopy a copy of the graphic organiser for each child.

Directions:
1. Explain to the class that some bugs have positive characteristics, for instance, bees pollinate flowers. However, other bugs cause problems. Mosquitoes bite people. Flies can be annoying. Termites eat the wood of houses.
2. Have the children use the graphic organisers to help focus on the assignment. They can choose their own insects or pick from the list on the graphic organiser.
3. Once the children have found two facts about an insect with annoying or harmful characteristics, have them describe these insects in a comic strip format. They can draw pictures of the insects and write the harmful characteristics beneath the pictures. Or they can use the insects as characters in a strip that also features bugs with positive characteristics.

Option:
• Hang the finished fact-filled pictures in the classroom.

Note:
• Younger children can dictate this assignment.
• Depending on their abilities, children can find more than two characteristics.

Did You Know...
People kill termites because termites eat wood. Termites can make a house fall down!

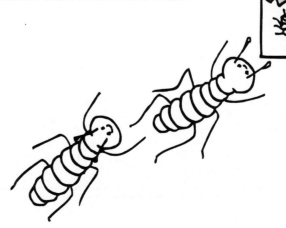

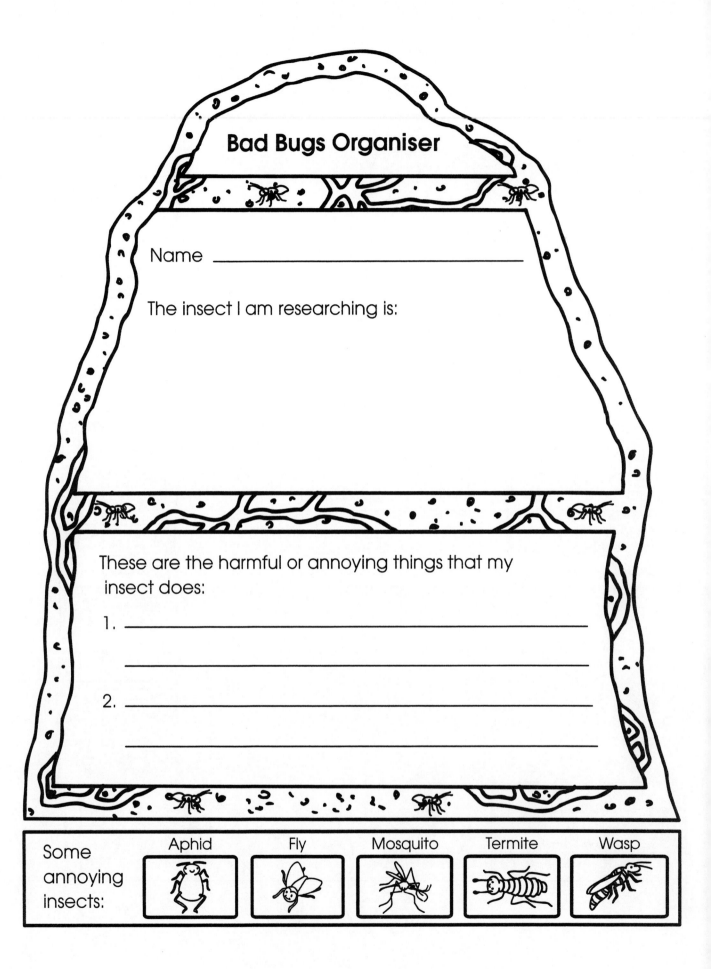

Bad Bugs Organiser

Name _____

The insect I am researching is:

These are the harmful or annoying things that my insect does:

1. _____

_____

2. _____

_____

Some annoying insects:	Aphid	Fly	Mosquito	Termite	Wasp

Lightning Bug Spelling

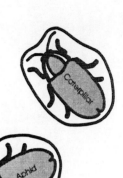

Materials:
Fireflies (p. 28), Jar (p. 29), bag, construction paper, scissors, coloured textas

Preparation:
1. Photocopy a copy of the Fireflies for each child and one for teacher use.
2. Cut one set of the bugs apart and colour as desired.
3. Enlarge the Jar pattern and hang on a bulletin board.

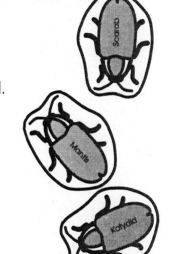

Directions:
1. Announce a date for a spelling "bee".
2. Describe fireflies for children who aren't familiar with them. If possible, show colour pictures of fireflies from a book.
3. Divide the students into small groups. Have the children work together to learn the words. Let the children take the Fireflies home to study. They can cut out the bugs and colour as desired.
4. On the day of the spelling bee, put the bugs in a bag. Pull one bug from the bag at a time and have a child from each group spell the word on the bug.
5. If the child spells the word correctly, he or she can hang the bug in the jar. If not, another child from that group tries to spell the word.
6. Continue until each child has a chance to spell one word and all of the bugs are hung on the board.

Option:
• Write additional spelling words in the blank bug.

Fireflies

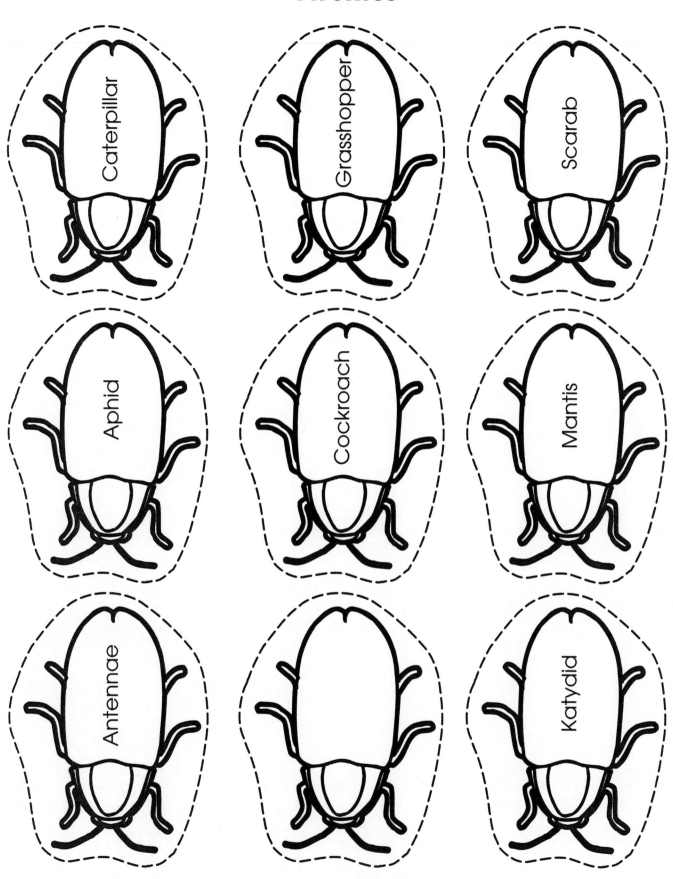

Jar

Beaded Bees

Beads have been used in art throughout the ages. However, even modern artists have been known to include beads in their artwork. This cooperative display will definitely brighten your classroom.

Materials:
Large sheet of paper, tempera paints, paintbrushes, heavy paper, scissors, glue, coloured beads, textas

Preparation:
None

Directions:
1. Explain that bees pollinate flowers as they gather nectar. Pollen sticks to their hind legs and is carried from one flower to the next.
2. Have the children paint a garden backdrop on the large paper using a variety of coloured paints.
3. While the backdrop dries, have each child draw a bee and a flower on a sheet of heavy paper and cut them out.
4. Provide a variety of coloured beads for the children to use to glue to their bees and flowers. They can cover their cutouts with beads or colour their cut-outs with textas and use the beads as finishing decorations.
5. Have the children hang their beaded bees and flowers on the painted backdrop to make a sparkling mural.

Did You Know...
Honeybees talk to each other. When a honeybee finds a flower with nectar, it tells the other bees about it. To do this, the bee does a special dance.

Pin the Spot on the Ladybird

Materials:
Red poster paper, black texta, black self-sticking dots, blindfold (optional)

Preparation:
Draw a large ladybird on the red poster paper.

Directions:
1. Discuss the fact that ladybirds are beetles. Beetles have two sets of wings. A hard, outer set protects the flying wings beneath.
2. Place the poster paper at an appropriate level on a wall.
3. Explain to the children that they will be playing a game that is similar to "pin the tail on the donkey".
4. Give the first child one self-sticking dot, and either blindfold the child or have the child close his or her eyes.
5. Have the children attempt to pin the spot on the ladybird.
6. Make sure each child has a chance to play the game.

Note:
• Save the finished gameboard for week three's maths activity.

> **Did You Know...**
> A ladybird spits yellow liquid to protect itself from enemies. The liquid smells and tastes bad!

Bee Song

Would You Like to Buzz Like a Bee?
(to the tune of "Swing on a Star?")

Would you like to buzz like a bee?
Carry pollen from tree to tree?
And be better off than a flea?
Oh, would you like to be a bee?

Would you like to fly like a fly?
Zoom across the sunny blue sky?
Stay away from spiders or die?
Oh, would you like to be a fly?

Would you like to eat lots of wood?
Just go munching through neighbourhoods?
And be mostly up to no good?
Would you be a termite if you could?

Would you like to light up the sky?
Like a brightly lit firefly?
And go flitting off way up high?
Oh, would you be a firefly?

Insect Concentration

Materials:
Concentration Cards (p. 34), scissors, crayons or textas

Preparation:
Photocopy two copies of the cards for each child.

Directions:
1. Give each child two copies of the cards to colour and cut out.
2. Teach the children the concentration game. They turn all of the cards face-down. Then they take turns flipping two cards over. If the pictures on the cards match, they keep both and try again. If the cards don't match, they turn them face-down and another child takes a turn.
3. The children can take the concentration game home to play with their families.

Option:
• Older children can practise spelling the names of the insects as they turn over the cards.

Concentration Cards

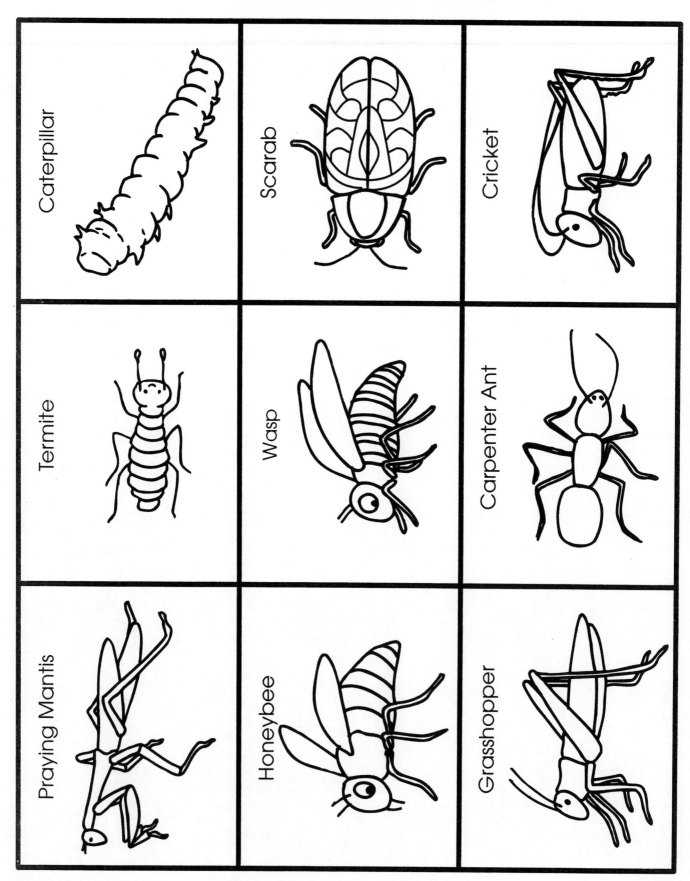

Caterpillar

Scarab

Cricket

Termite

Wasp

Carpenter Ant

Praying Mantis

Honeybee

Grasshopper

Mary Had a Little Bug

Materials:
Mother Goose Rhymes (p. 36), paper, pens or pencils, books of Mother Goose or other children's rhymes

Preparation:
Photocopy a copy of the rhymes for each child.

Directions:
1. Read the rhymes with the students.
2. Explain that the children will be rewriting the rhymes to feature insects. Work together as a class to rewrite at least one rhyme.
3. Let the children each choose rhymes to rewrite. They can choose from those on the sheet or from books of rhymes. Explain that it is easiest to simply replace words inside a rhyme—so that the rhyme itself stays the same. Children can experiment with different rhymes.
4. Hold a poetry reading in which the children recite their rewritten rhymes.

Options:
• Let the children work together in pairs or small groups.
• Provide rhyming dictionaries.
• Have children work to include facts in their rhymes.

Examples:
Mary had a little bug.
Its shell was hard and red.
It followed Mary home from school,
And slept upon her bed.

Twinkle, twinkle, firefly,
Shining bright as you fly by.
Up above the moon so high,
Like a diamond in the sky,
Twinkle, twinkle, firefly,
Shining bright as you fly by.

Mother Goose Rhymes

Peter, Peter, Pumpkin Eater
Peter, Peter, pumpkin eater
Had a wife, but couldn't keep her.
Put her in a pumpkin shell,
And there he kept her, very well.

Wee Willy Winkie
Wee Willy Winkie
Runs through the town.
Upstairs, downstairs, in his nightgown.
Rapping at the windows, crying through the locks,
Are the children all in bed, for now it's eight o'clock!

Mistress Mary
Mistress Mary, quite contrary,
How does your garden grow?
With silver bells, and cockle shells,
And pretty maids all in a row.

Simple Simon Met a Pie Man
Simple Simon met a pie man
Going to the fair.
Said Simple Simon to the pie man,
"Let me taste your ware."
Said the pie man to Simple Simon,
"Show me first your penny."
Said Simple Simon to the pie man,
"Indeed, I have not any."

Jack and Jill
Jack and Jill went up a hill
To fetch a pail of water.
Jack fell down and broke
        his crown,
And Jill fell tumbling after.

Ladybird Lessons

Materials:
Ladybird Poster from "Pin the Spot on the Ladybird" (p. 31), pushpins or sticky tape, paper, pencils

Preparation:
None

Directions:
1. Hang the Ladybird Poster where all of the children can see it.
2. Have the children count the number of dots on the ladybird's shell.
3. Make up several maths problems based on the number of dots on the ladybird. For instance, if there are 10 dots on the one side of the ladybird's shell and 15 on the other, have the children add the numbers to get a total. Do several problems as a class.
4. Challenge the children to make up maths problems for each other based on the dots. They can draw pictures to accompany the problems (as shown in the margin). Have them make up answer keys, as well. (Based on the level of the children's abilities, have them make up addition, subtraction, or multiplication problems. Also assign them a number of problems to create.)
5. Check the children's work, then let the children switch papers and try each other's problems.

Did You Know...
Ladybirds are called the "gardener's friend" because they eat aphids.

Insect Stages

Butterflies go through complete metamorphosis. They start as eggs, which hatch into larvae. The larva goes through a pupal stage before turning into an adult.

Materials:
Life Stages Cards (p. 39), crayons, textas, glue, construction paper, scissors

Preparation:
Photocopy a copy of the cards for each child.

Directions:
1. Give each child a copy of the cards to colour and cut apart.
2. Describe the process by which a caterpillar turns into a butterfly. Go over the steps with the children.

> Step one: The mother insect lays an egg
> Step two: Larva hatches (butterfly larva is a caterpillar)
> Step three: Larva goes through inactive pupal stage
> Step four: Adult emerges (adult is the butterfly)

3. Have the children match the picture cards with the facts. They can then glue the cards in correct order on a large sheet of coloured construction paper (with the pictures above the facts). Or they can make insect stages books, putting the pictures and facts on facing pages. Children can also make their own books, drawing their own versions of the pictures and writing or dictating their own text. They can add other facts, as well.

Book Link:
• *The Very Hungry Caterpillar* by Eric Carle (Puffin, 1987).

> **Did You Know...**
> The pupal stage for an insect can last from four days to several months! It depends on the type of insect.

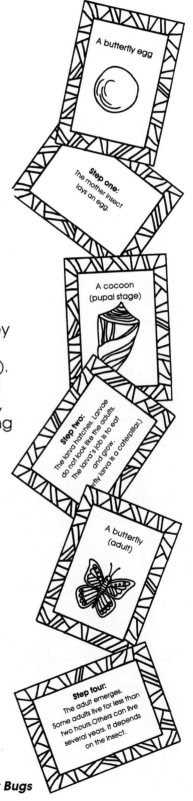

A butterfly egg

Step one:
The mother insect lays an egg.

A cocoon (pupal stage)

Step two:
The larva hatches. Larvae do not look like the adults. The larva's job is to eat and grow. (A butterfly larva is a caterpillar.)

A butterfly (adult)

Step four:
The adult emerges. Some adults live for less than two hours. Others can live several years. It depends on the insect.

Life Stages Cards

A butterfly egg

A caterpillar (larva stage)

A cocoon (pupal stage)

A butterfly (adult)

Step one:
The mother insect lays an egg.

Step two:
The larva hatches. Larvae do not look like the adults. The larva's job is to eat and grow.
(Butterfly larva is a caterpillar.)

Step three:
Larva goes through a pupal stage in a cocoon. The cocoon is a protective case. A great change happens during this stage.

Step four:
The adult emerges. Some adults live for less than two hours. Others can live several years. It depends on the insect.

Butterfly Behaviour

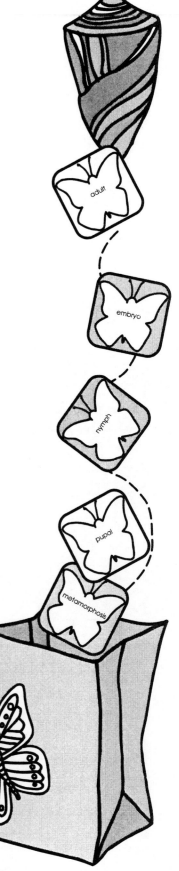

Materials:
Butterflies (p. 41), Cocoon (p. 42), bag, construction paper, scissors, coloured textas

Preparation:
1. Photocopy a copy of the Butterflies for each child and one for teacher use.
2. Cut one set of the Butterflies apart and colour as desired.
3. Enlarge the Cocoon pattern and hang on a bulletin board.

Directions:
1. Announce a date for a spelling "bee".
2. Divide the students into small groups. Have the children work together to learn the words.
3. Let the children take the Butterflies home to study. They can cut them out and colour them as desired.
4. On the day of the spelling bee, put the bugs in a bag. Pull one bug from the bag at a time and have a child from each group spell the word on the bug.
5. If the child spells the word correctly, he or she can hang the butterfly near the cocoon. If not, another child from that group tries to spell the word.
6. Continue until each child has a chance to spell one word and all of the bugs are hung on the board.

Options:
• Write additional spelling words in the blank butterflies.
• Use the more difficult words, such as metamorphosis, for bonus spelling words. Younger children often like to learn how to say difficult words.
• Make mobiles from the butterflies by punching a hole in each one and suspending from the bottom of a hanger.
• Have children learn definitions for each spelling word.

Butterflies

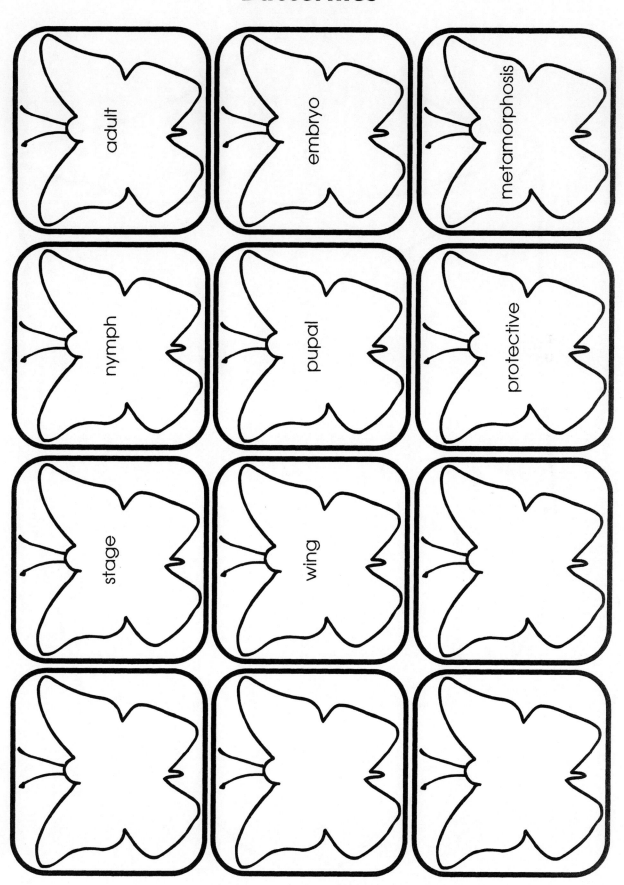

adult

embryo

metamorphosis

nymph

pupal

protective

stage

wing

Cocoon

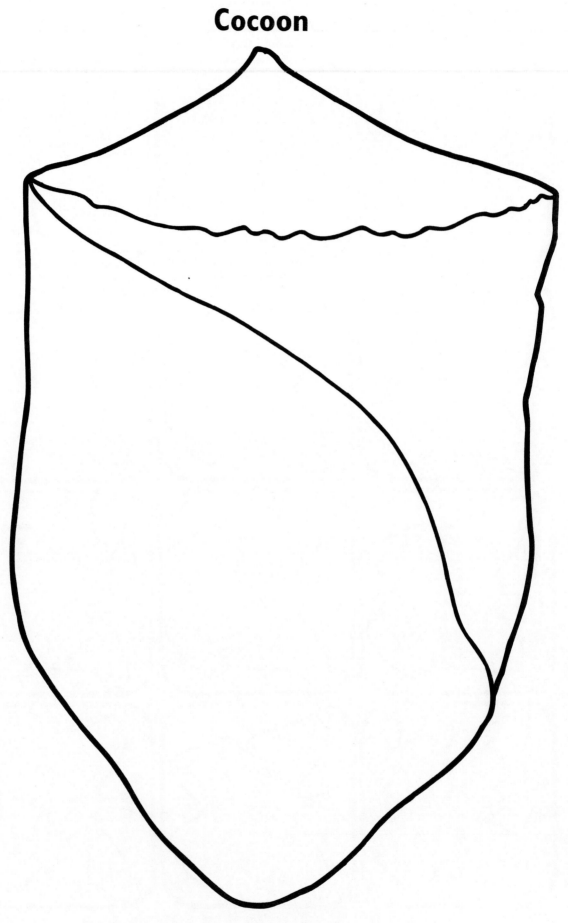

Mâché Metamorphosis

Materials:
Newspaper, water, flour, paintbrushes, tempera paints, containers, scissors, sheets of paper, crayons or textas

Preparation:
1. Mix the water and flour together to make a thin paste.
2. Shred the newspaper into long strands.

Directions:
1. Cover the work area with extra newspaper.
2. Demonstrate the art of papier-mâché. Crumple a ball of paper for the base. Dip strips of newspaper into the paste and cover the crumpled paper.
3. Explain that the children will be making papier-mâché representations of insect metamorphosis. They will make small eggs, thin caterpillars, and cocoons.
4. When the children finish making the papier-mâché, they should let their creations dry. During this phase, they can make large paper butterflies.
5. When the papier-mâché is dry, the children can paint the eggs, caterpillars, and cocoons.
6. Display the four stages of butterfly metamorphosis near books about insects.

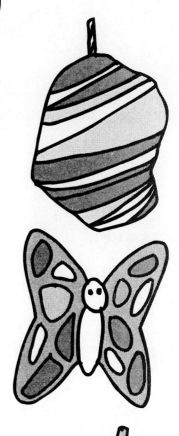

Who Wants to be an Entomologist?

Entomology is the study of insects. Children will challenge each other with multiple-choice questions to share what they know about entomology.

Materials:
Quiz Questions (p. 45), index cards, pencils, resource books about insects

Preparation:
None

Directions:
1. Explain the game. You will read off a question and four possible answers. Children who think they know the answer will raise their hands. Choose one to answer. If he or she is correct, let this child read the next question. If not, keep going until a child answers correctly.
2. Once the children understand the game, have each child create his or her own question with four possible answers. The children should write the question and answers on one side of an index card and the correct answer on the back. They can use information from this book or from resource books about insects. Be sure to explain that three of the answers should be incorrect and only one will be correct.
3. Gather all of the children's questions and continue with the quiz game. Or let the children quiz each other.

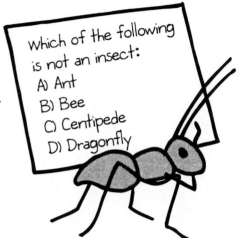

Which of the following is not an insect:
A) Ant
B) Bee
C) Centipede
D) Dragonfly

Options:
• Let the children have a chance to remove two incorrect answers.
• Allow children to confer with a friend about the correct answer.

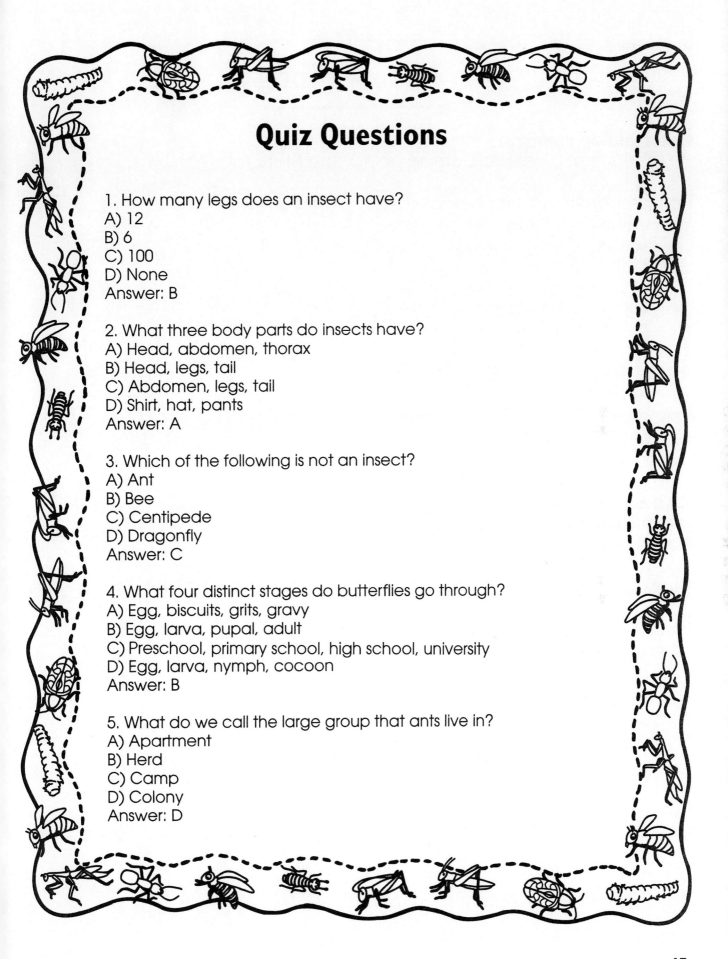

Quiz Questions

1. How many legs does an insect have?
A) 12
B) 6
C) 100
D) None
Answer: B

2. What three body parts do insects have?
A) Head, abdomen, thorax
B) Head, legs, tail
C) Abdomen, legs, tail
D) Shirt, hat, pants
Answer: A

3. Which of the following is not an insect?
A) Ant
B) Bee
C) Centipede
D) Dragonfly
Answer: C

4. What four distinct stages do butterflies go through?
A) Egg, biscuits, grits, gravy
B) Egg, larva, pupal, adult
C) Preschool, primary school, high school, university
D) Egg, larva, nymph, cocoon
Answer: B

5. What do we call the large group that ants live in?
A) Apartment
B) Herd
C) Camp
D) Colony
Answer: D

Butterfly Song

Caterpillar to Butterfly
(to the tune of "She'll Be Coming 'round the Mountain")

He'll be hatching from an egg when morning comes,
Yes, he'll be hatching from an egg
    when morning comes,
He'll be hatching from an egg,
Yes, he'll be hatching from an egg,
Oh, he'll be hatching from an egg
    when morning comes.

Then he'll live life as a larva in the sun,
Yes, he'll live life as a larva in the sun,
Eating green leaves, oh, you know,
Because the larva has to grow,
Oh, he'll be living as a larva in the sun.

For the pupal stage, he'll be in a cocoon,
For the pupal stage, he'll be in a cocoon,
From the morning until noon,
And at night under the bright moon,
During the pupal stage, he'll be in a cocoon.

When he emerges, well you won't believe your eyes.
When he emerges, oh, you won't believe your eyes.
As an adult, well, he flies,
    and you just won't believe your eyes,
Because he'll be a big and lovely butterfly.

Insect Camouflage

Materials:
Insects (p. 48), scissors

Preparation:
Photocopy a copy of the Insects patterns for each child.

Directions:
1. Discuss the fact that different insects use camouflage as a means to survive. Their shape or colouring helps them blend into their surroundings. For instance, many grasshoppers blend with grass because they are green or brown. Some insects look like leaves or sticks.
2. Give each child a sheet of Insects patterns. Have the children cut-out the patterns and take them home. They should colour the patterns at home so that the insects will blend with their new environment. If a child hangs a grasshopper on his or her blue bedroom wall, he or she should colour the insect blue.
3. Have the children bring back their coloured insects and describe how the insects blended with their surroundings at home.
4. Hang the coloured insects in the classroom so that all of the children can see how their classmates coloured their insects. This will give students an idea about the many different types of environments that real insects have to blend with in the world.

Option:
• Show the children pictures of camouflaged insects from books.

> **Did You Know...**
> Some bugs camouflage themselves to look like their poisonous relatives, even though they aren't poisonous themselves. This keeps birds and other prey from eating them.

Insects

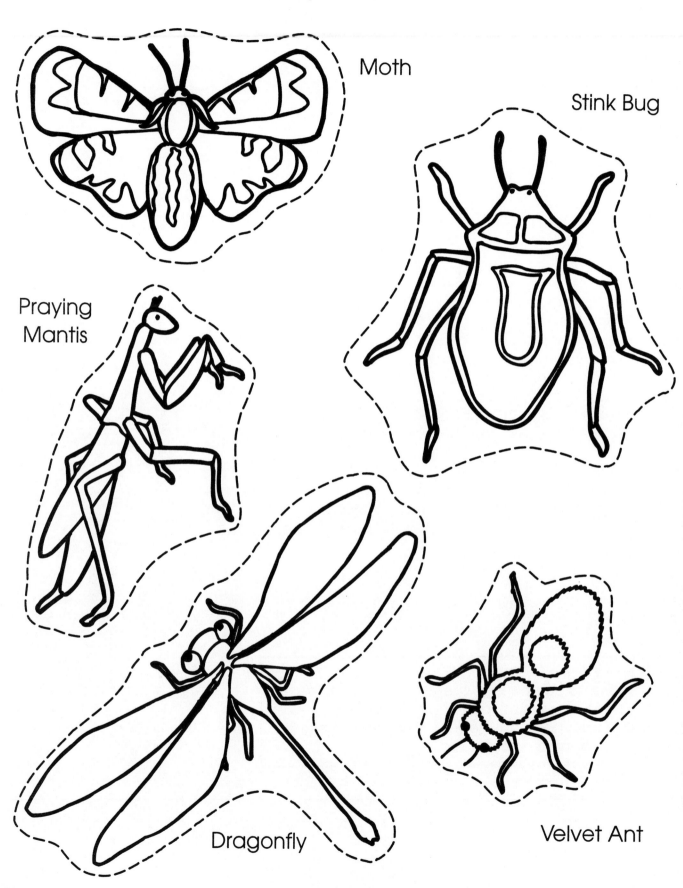

Moth

Stink Bug

Praying Mantis

Dragonfly

Velvet Ant

Calming Miss Muffet

Little Miss Muffet is famous for being frightened away by a spider. In this activity, the children will explain to Miss Muffet why spiders are useful creatures.

Materials:
Books about spiders, paper, pens or pencils

Preparation:
Gather together resource books about spiders.

Directions:
1. Recite the poem "Little Miss Muffet" to the children.
2. Have the children research to find out reasons why spiders are useful. For instance, spiders eat other bugs.
3. Explain to the children that they will be writing messages to Miss Muffet, calming her fears of spiders. Consider giving children an example, such as:

> Dear Little Miss Muffet,
>   Please don't run away the next time a spider approaches. Spiders can be very helpful to humans. They eat bugs such as mosquitoes.
>   Sincerely,
>   A fan of spiders

4. Hang the completed messages on a bulletin board near books about spiders.

Note:
• Point out that some spiders are poisonous, and that the children should never handle or touch any spiders.

Super Spider Maths

This activity can be used for different levels of maths study. For younger children, write a plus or minus sign in the middle fly of each equation. Write in a multiplication sign for older children.

Materials:
Watch the Webs (p. 51), pencils

Preparation:
1. Fill in the missing signs (+, -, or x), then photocopy the Watch the Webs page. Make one for each child.
2. Make an answer key for self-checking, if desired.

Directions:
1. Give each child a copy of the Watch the Webs page.
2. Have the children do the problems and then share their answers with the class. Or they can use the answer key for self-checking.

Options:
• For older children, pass out the Watch the Webs page without any signs written in the middle flies. Let the children make their own problems. They can add a +, -, or x and then write the answers on the back. Have the children trade papers.
• To make the problems more difficult, white-out the numbers on the flies and write in your own numerals.

Did You Know...
Spiders, unlike insects, have no antennae.

Watch the Webs

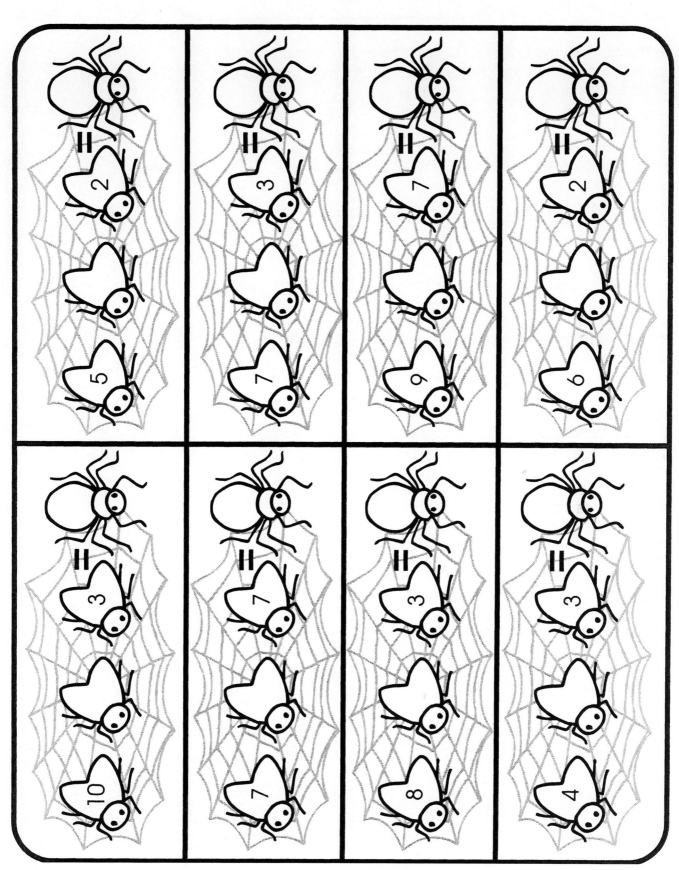

Eight-Legged Reports

In this activity, the children research to learn descriptions of spiders. If possible, provide an assortment of materials for the children to study.

Materials:
Spider (p. 53), books about spiders (include encyclopedias, magazines, or Web research), paper, pens or pencils

Preparation:
Gather books about spiders.

Directions:
1. Have the children research spiders. They should write down different facts that they find interesting.
2. Give each child a spider pattern.
3. Have the children choose the most important spider-related eight words from their research. For instance, they might choose: web, legs, spinnerets, pincers, arachnid, hairy, tiny, silk. Each child may choose different words that he or she thinks best describe a spider.
4. Have the children write the eight words on the spider pattern's eight legs.
5. Hang the completed spiders on a bulletin board.

Option:
• Older children might write whole facts or phrases on the spider's legs.

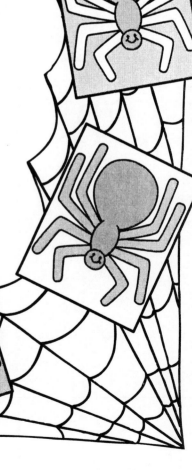

Spider

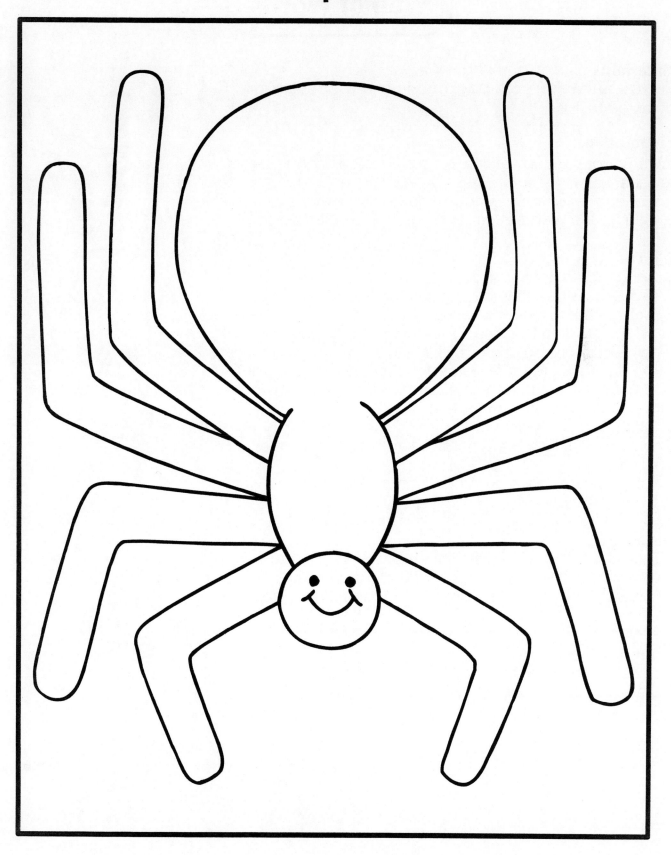

53

Web of Words

Materials:
Flies (p. 55), Web (p. 56), bag, construction paper, scissors, coloured textas

Preparation:
1. Photocopy a copy of the Flies for each child and one for teacher use.
2. Cut one set of the flies apart and colour as desired.
3. Enlarge the Web pattern and hang on a bulletin board.

Directions:
1. Announce a date for a spelling "bee".
2. Divide the students into small groups. Have the children work together to learn the words.
3. Let the children take the flies home to study. They can cut them out and colour them as desired.
4. On the day of the spelling bee, put the flies in a bag. Pull one fly from the bag at a time and have a child from each group spell the word on the fly.
5. If the child spells the word correctly, he or she can hang the fly on the web. If not, another child from that group tries to spell the word.
6. Continue until each child has a chance to spell one word and all of the flies are hung on the board.

Options:
• Trace the web using silver glitter glue to make it sparkle.
• Write an additional spelling word in the blank fly.
• Have children learn definitions for each spelling word.

Did You Know...
Spiders are related to scorpions, ticks, and mites.

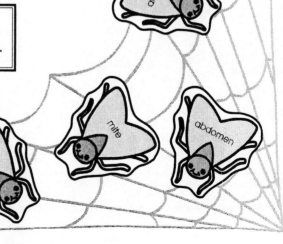

Flies

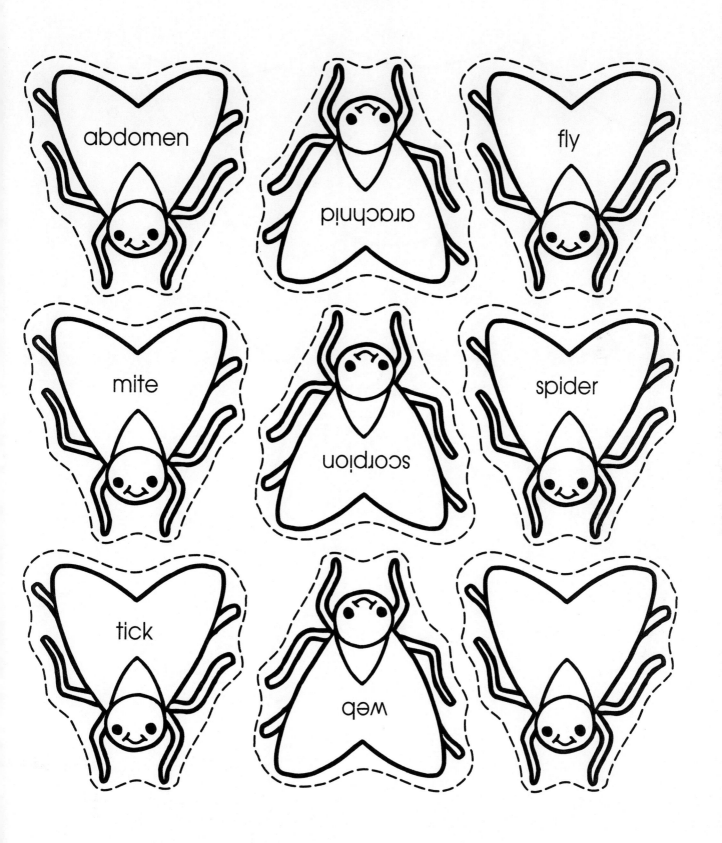

Web

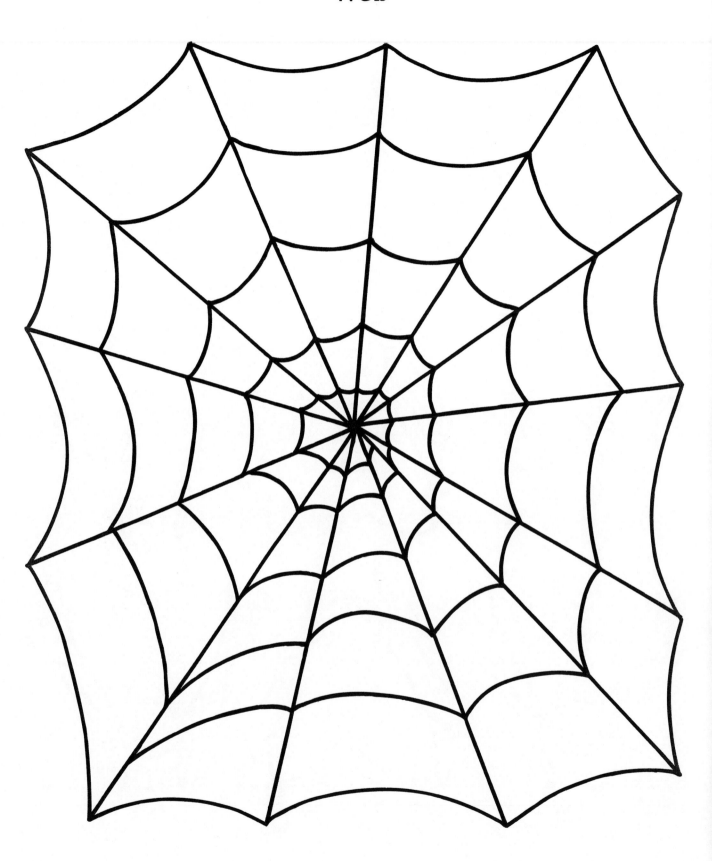

Web Weaving

Materials:
Blank flies (p. 55), scissors, construction paper in different colours, glue, black wool, pipe-cleaners

Preparation:
Photocopy the flies so that each child can have at least one.

Directions:
1. Demonstrate this activity for the children. Cut a large sheet of construction paper into a web shape (a circle or an octagon works well). Then cut slits into the paper that go almost to the edge without cutting through. Cut a different coloured sheet of construction paper into thin strips. Weave the strips through the web.
2. Once children have woven webs, let them glue one or more flies to their webs.
3. Children can make simple spiders from black wool—four pieces of wool wrapped around the middle with a short piece of pipe-cleaner. They can hang the spiders from their webs or glue them directly to the webs.

Option:
• Have the children write facts about spiders on their flies.

> **Did You Know...**
> Spiders spin webs to catch food. The web traps insects, which the spider eats.

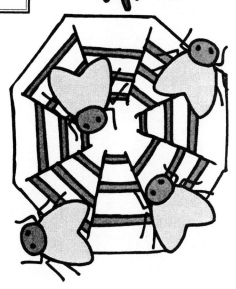

Wheel of Wonder

Materials:
Wheel (p. 59), resource books about insects and spiders, heavy paper, paper fasteners, hole punch, glue, scissors

Preparation:
1. Photocopy and enlarge the Wheel and mount onto heavy paper.
2. Attach the spinner to the Wheel using a paper fastener.

Directions:
1. Explain the game to the children. One child spins the wheel. He or she looks at the segment the spinner landed on and decides whether the characteristic is one that a spider has or one that an insect has.
2. Once all of the answers have been given, let the children make their own wheels. They can include pictures or written facts. Then they can test their friends' insect and spider knowledge.

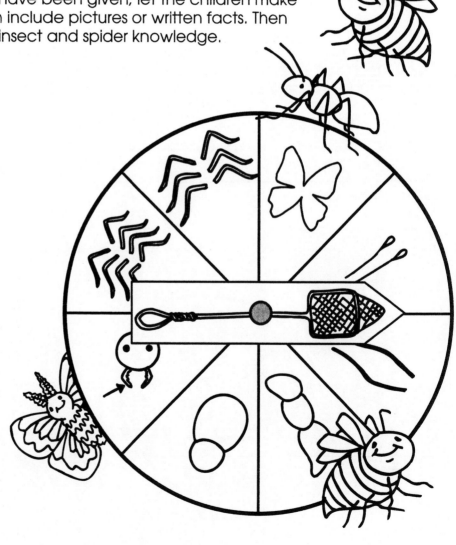

Wheel

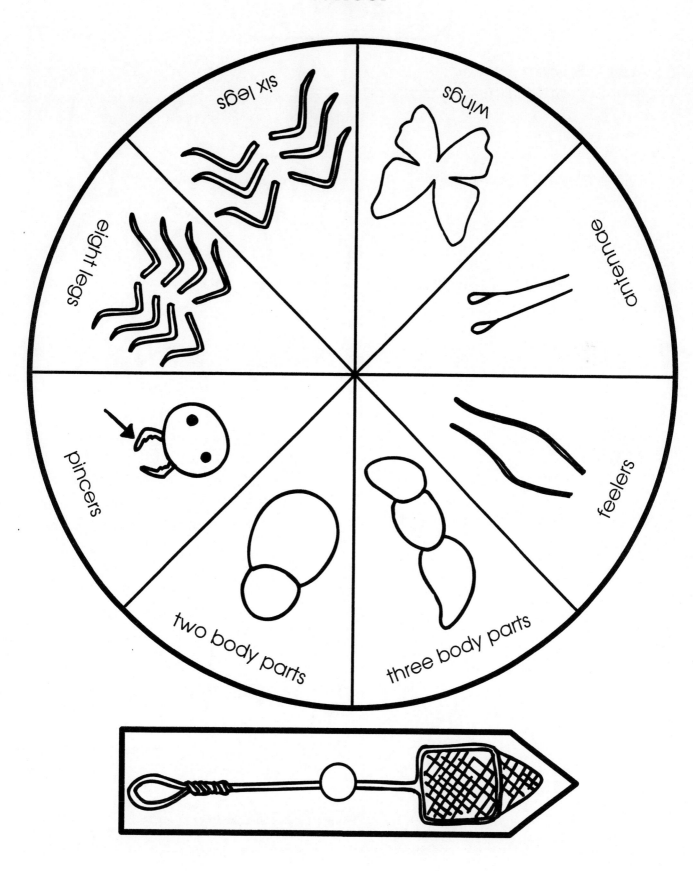

Spider Songs

If I Were a Spider
(to the tune of "If I Had a Hammer")

If I were a spider,
I'd spin webs in the morning,
I'd spin webs in the evening,
All over this land.
I'd spin some circles,
I'd spin some ovals,
I'd spin my webs to catch
      some insects for my dinner,
All over this land.

I'm a Spider
(to the tune of "Alouette")

I'm a spider,
Yes, I am a spider,
I'm a spider,
I'm an arachnid.
I'm related to a mite
Don't you think that's out of sight?
To a mite, to a mite,
Out of sight, out of sight.
Oh, I'm a spider,
Yes, I am a spider,
I'm a spider,
I'm an arachnid.

Spotting Spiders

Explain to the children not to disturb any spiders that they see. Their goal is simply to be aware of spiders in the world around them.

Materials:
Spider Tally (p. 62), pens or pencils

Preparation:
Photocopy a copy of the Spotting Spiders sheet for each child.

Directions:
1. Give each child a copy of the Spotting Spiders sheet to take home.
2. Have the children make notes every time they see a spider for a set amount of days, such as a weekend. The children should note where the spiders were—for instance, outdoors in a bush, inside the house, attached to a web.
3. Have the children bring back their sheets to compare their information with the other students.

Options:
• Have the children draw pictures of the different spiders they see. Then use resource books to identify the spiders.
• Have children observe other insects and their habitats.

SPIDER TALLY

Spiders I Saw (Color a spider each time you see one.)	Where I saw the spiders. List where you saw each spider.
🕷	I saw a spider under my desk.
🕷	
🕷	
🕷	
🕷	
🕷	
🕷	
🕷	
🕷	

SPIDER TALLY

Spiders I Saw (Colour a spider each time you see one.)	Where I saw the spiders. List where you saw each spider.

Insect Book Links

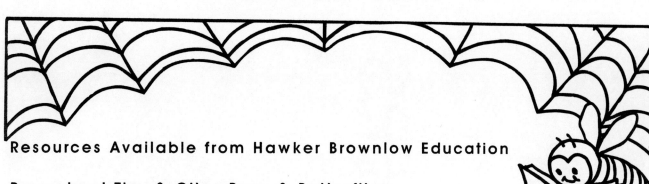

Resources Available from Hawker Brownlow Education

Pre-school Tips & Clips Bugs & Butterflies
Marilynn G. Barr • ISBN 1 74025 896 7

Ladybird, Ladybird - Super Duper Science
Annalisa Suid • ISBN 1 74025 885 1

DK Eyewitness Guides Butterfly & Moth
Simon James • ISBN 0 86318 319 0

DK Eyewitness Guides Insect
Simon James • ISBN 0 86318 408 1

Incredible Insects - Super Duper Science (Years 1–3)
Annalisa Suid • ISBN 1 74025 769 3

Inquiry Science: Mini Beasts: Invertebrates (Years 4–5)
Marcia Hildebrand & Lara Parent Johnson • ISBN 1 74025 163 6

Insects - Super Science Activities (Years 3–6)
Ruth M Young • ISBN 1 74025 746 4

Bugs 'n' Stuff (Years 3–6)
Kaye Quinn • ISBN 0 94732 679 0

Learning Cards Insects
Instructional Fair • ISBN 1 74025 666 2

Self-Directed Learning Units – Science: Entomology (Years 3–7)
Clements, Domin and Tanner • ISBN 1 86299 979 1

Thematic Unit: Life Cycles
ISBN 1 86401 770 8

Collecting Bugs and Things
Julia Spencer Moutran • ISBN 1 86299 082

Integrated Unit: Mini Beasts
Jennifer Overend Prior • ISBN 1 74025 046 X

Insect Diploma

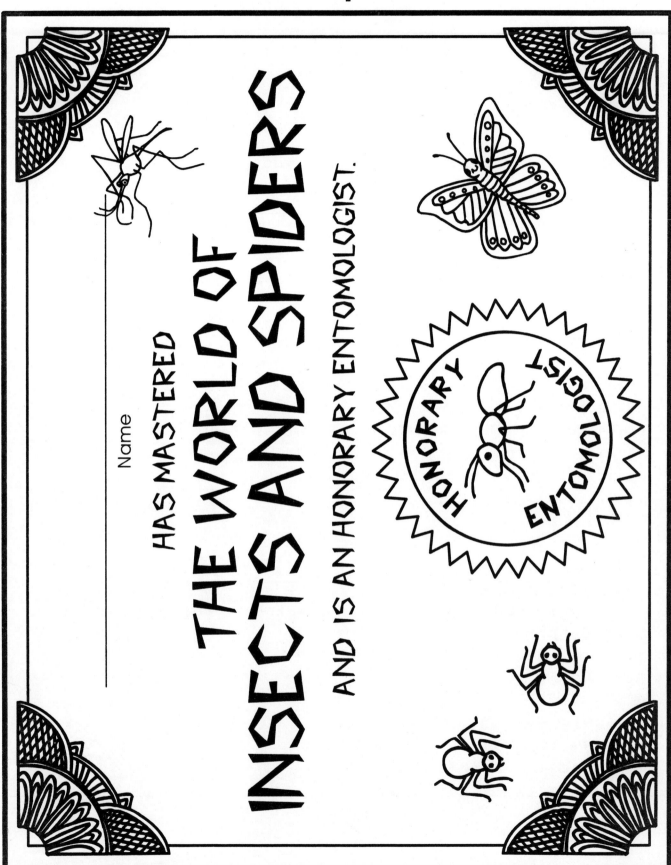

Name

HAS MASTERED

THE WORLD OF INSECTS AND SPIDERS

AND IS AN HONORARY ENTOMOLOGIST.

HONORARY ENTOMOLOGIST

The Gospel and *Tomorrow's Culture*

Graham Cray

C O N T E N T S

Nowhere But Now 3

What's Your World View? 9

Pick 'n' Mix at the Pluralist Superstore 17

Telling Your Story..25

Communities of Hope 35

Introduction

We live in a fast-changing world. Our gospel remains the same, yet the way we present it to others needs to take into account how people think and react today.

This is a practical book. Its focus is the culture of today and tomorrow, so that through understanding we may be more effective in our presentation of the gospel. We need to know how we can communicate eternal truths in our throw-away society.

Some will want to read this book by themselves. However, the exercises make it an invaluable study for small groups. It is not a structured course, but the five chapters will take any group through an understanding of our modern, complex culture to an appreciation of the power of telling our own stories of faith. The culture of today and tomorrow is only the backdrop against which the Church seeks faithfully to proclaim the Good News of Christ crucified and risen. As Bishop Michael Marshall has said,

'The Christian has three stories to tell: the story of the Bible, the story of their own encounter with God, but supremely the story of Jesus.'

Copyright and photocopying

The material in this book is © 1994 Graham Cray and CPAS and may not be copied without permission. However, permission is given for the owner of this book to copy pages for use in study or discussion groups in which he or she is participating.

Acknowledgements

The exercises on pages 7-8, 32-33 and 40 are adapted from resource sheets published by The Media Awareness Project and are used by their kind permission. MAP is an ecumenical project promoting media awareness and offering resource material, workshop/conference programmes and a consultancy function. MAP is supported by the Mothers' Union. Further details and a list of resources may be obtained from:

Jane Harvey
The Media Awareness Project
24 Tufton Street
LONDON
SW1P 3RB

Tel: 071-233 1887

Nowhere But Now

As the year 2000 comes into view, more and more people are feeling that our century has failed to deliver all that it promised.

With so many disenchanted people, shouldn't there be a ready audience for what the Church wants to say? You would certainly think so – and it is true that if you listen you'll hear many questioning voices. But beyond the voices I detect something truly frightening – silence.

Most people have no sense of crisis. Of course we react to news of disaster and terrorist outrage but when horror becomes the staple diet of our news bulletins, it's inevitable that we become increasingly immune to it and distanced from it. It's on telly so it doesn't affect us! We don't recognize the crisis we are in. We are numb.

Loss of the past – loss of the future

I believe there is a reason for this: we've lost hold of the past – and we've no grip on the future.

What's happened? For the past 250 years we have believed in progress – that today is better than yesterday and that tomorrow will be better still. Because we've valued what's modern, we've come to despise the lessons and values of the past, arrogantly judging our culture superior to those which came before us. As a result we are rootless.

All this seemed fine while we believed in progress, but now we appear to have lost hope in our ability to make a better world. At best the future has become unsure.

With no sense of rootedness in yesterday, and no real confidence in a better tomorrow, there's only one place left: the present.

> 66 Our era has been united by current technologies into an instantaneous 24-hour information world. 99
> Charles Jencks *What is Post-Modernism?*

Here and now

Many people today live for the present because that is all they feel sure of. They're wearing blinkers, with both the past and future out of sight. Their isolation is made all the more acute because they have to live without a shared set of values. There is a growing acceptance that the standards by which we judge what is right and wrong are matters of private interpretation – a DIY morality.

'... a DIY morality.'

We are busy filling the present, keeping ourselves numb without knowing it. But with what? Here's a brief list:

☐ *With material goods* It's been said that we've nowhere left to go but to the shops. Shopping is considered to be our most popular leisure activity, 'the primary cultural pursuit of the twentieth century'. Our gleaming shopping malls are our new cathedrals, and people want to worship on a Sunday!

> 66 In the laboratory I make cosmetics, in the store I sell dreams. 99
> Charles Revlon, founder of Revlon Cosmetics

We've become a 'commodity culture'. We have little hope of a better future but we want the good life now. Our acquisitive lifestyle shows that we believe the opposite of the words of Jesus: that our life *does* consist in what we possess. We always want more, but somehow it's the buying rather than the having that has become important. Our culture is not so much greedy as disillusioned. We don't believe there is anything else so we make the most of the shops.

☐ *With images* Time was when our culture was book-based. Now it's a screen culture — TV, video and computer screens are the main forms of communication.

> 66 In the Canadian film *Jesus of Montreal*, the Jesus figure goes into the TV studio rather than the temple and overthrows the lights and cameras. 99
> Duncan Forrester *Discerning Images*

Children's magazines are laid out for screen watchers — you scan them, rather than read them from beginning to end like a book. The same is true of tabloid newspapers.

'Our gleaming shopping malls are our new cathedrals.'

Almost anything from any age or culture can be brought into your front room. It is an overwhelming bombardment — image after image — but it's all fragmented. The screen lifts everything out of its full context. It has to, that is the way TV works. But the result is to reinforce the sense of a permanent present. Everybody in the electronic age lives in a world in which all events occur at the same time.

I wonder if you've noticed two new items of political jargon: *photo-opportunity* and *sound-bite*. We've all seen that so-authoritative shot of the candidate against an impressive background, and heard that so-pithy statement that will ensure inclusion in the first minutes of the evening TV news. It's all pictures and words manipulated from their context to serve the new agenda of persuasion, building images rather than communicating policies.

And where do image, persuasion and shopping meet? In advertising. It has been called the 'principal medium of the new culture' and it's the place where some of our most talented and creative communicators are employed.

Second for second, the amount of money spent on TV commercials far outstrips what is spent on most programmes. So when your friend asks 'Did you see...?' she's just as likely to be talking about a new advertisement as about a new programme.

***

" A survey by the advertising agency McCann Erickson showed that when asked what makes for happiness, British teenagers put money above friends and love. 'Choice has become increasingly important,' their report said, 'and consumption is one route towards establishing identity and individuality. "

***

Advertising invades more and more of life, particularly for young people. Pop concerts have commercial sponsorship; pop stars and sports personalities have advertising deals with soft drinks companies; cartoon series are sponsored by toy manufacturers; and both tee-shirts and designer clothing turn us into walking advertisements. Parents experience a double pressure as their children also bombard them for the latest training shoes or whatever.

☐ *With experiences* While there is still a strong feeling of community in many rural (and urban) villages, most of us have little sense of close-knit 'belonging'. We have never lived so close together and never been so lonely. And so we use *events* to create a sense of community. Whether it's at a football match, on a protest march or with a charity pop concert, there's an underlying yearning for having something in common with others, to break out of our isolation. But such events rarely lead to relationships based on shared values.

With a loss of community it's hardly surprising that personal relationships become devalued. Sexual experiences come to be a substitute for lasting intimacy. For many people, the opposite (or same) sex are just raw material for private sensation: 'you exist merely to make me feel good.' We've turned people into things.

***

" Creativity is no longer what we make, or what we think, but what we buy. "
Robert Hewison *Future Tense*

***

Surprisingly, for an increasing number, spiritual experience is becoming more important. Our culture is far less secular than we imagine. In fact sociologists no longer call Western society secular, they call it 'religiously pluralist'. Spiritual experience, prayer, meditation, healing or guidance can now be part of public as well as private life. Whether it's management training, cancer care, alternative medicine or courses on prayer and meditation, we've punctured a hole in the blinkers. But any and every spiritual experience is accepted (with the possible exception of traditional Christianity) and we have no ground rules for distinguishing the good from the bad or the barmy.

CHAPTER ONE

But we're not giving up wearing the blinkers. If anything, we have traded one pair of blinkers for another. Our 'permanent present' culture believes in feelings for feelings' sake, including spiritual feelings. No links are made between spiritual experiences and moral change. A survey of students showed that their key question about Christianity was not, 'Is it true?' or 'Does it work?', but 'Do I like it, and would I feel comfortable with it?' Truth has been reduced to whatever feels OK for the moment.

Even the Church has not escaped. It's a trend that is closer to home than you would think. I find it worrying that in many of our churches there are people who enjoy experiences of the Holy Spirit every Sunday, but they are experiences which seem to have very little impact on their behaviour Monday to Saturday. The experience itself is all that matters, and precious few connections are made with the rest of that person's life. All that matters is the spiritual feel-good factor.

57 varieties of choice

So we pump the present full with images, events and experiences. And what's the basic underlying value? I'm convinced that, above anything else, we've come to cherish what we see as our right to have freedom of choice.

66 The super-industrial revolution forces the whole problem of overchoice to a qualitatively new level. It forces us now to make choices not merely among lamps and lampshades, but among lives, not among life-style *components*, but among whole life *styles*. **99**
Alvin Toffler *Future Shock*

Whether it's roller blinds, ravioli or religion – what matters most is that I should be able to choose the variety that suits me. Sadly what fits the individual for now is the limit of our vision.

The Hidden Persuaders

AIM *To encourage participants to become 'advertisement conscious' and to compare the values behind advertisements with those encouraged in the Bible.*

PART 1 Ask members of the group to bring with them a range of advertisements from any sources – glossy magazines, newspapers, small advertisements, house agents, teenage magazines, etc. Place around the room labels marked with some of the following words: *femininity, comfort, acquisition, glamour, snobbery, fear, manliness, power, contentment, maternity, ambition, greed, status.*

Ask people to try to place their advertisements by the appropriate label. Those which do not seem to fit anywhere may form another section, but almost all advertisements appeal to one or more of the attributes/instincts listed above.

When all the advertisements are placed and any ensuing discussion has petered out, choose two or three words from the list to look at in detail. Ask the group how the advertisers use this attribute/instinct to 'push' their product. For example, many advertisements work on natural *fears*, such as the fear of growing old, not being popular or attractive, failing as a partner or mother, 'losing out' generally....

PART 2 Redistribute the advertisements and set out a different set of labels, this time from Paul's letter to the Galatians: *love, joy, peace, patience, kindness, goodness, faithfulness, humility, self-control.* Read out Galatians 5:16-24. Ask people to try to place the advertisements in the new categories.

☐ Come together and talk about the difficulty in matching the two sets of labels.

☐ Advertising often plays on human weaknesses – are there aspects of our Christian message which *also* relate to the advertisers' values?

☐ Is it right to appeal to people's needs when presenting the gospel? Where is the balance between seeing Jesus as a person's 'solution' or help line, rather than as King and Lord?

News Presentation

AIM *To encourage participants to realize how we are affected by the way stories are presented and to work on making a Bible story come alive.*

PART 1 The person leading the group should collect copies of different newspapers from one day and select a story which is covered by all the newspapers. The story should be of general interest, and something about which the group will be fairly knowledgeable.

Divide the group and give each sub-group a different newspaper. How would they cover the story for a major TV news bulletin? What would the pictures look like — close ups, long shots etc.? What sort of interviews would they have and with whom? What would the presenter say to introduce the story to the general public? (You may wish to narrow the audience, for example, to teenagers or women.)

Bring the groups back together and discuss:

☐ Which aspect of the story did they play up, which down?
☐ Which pictures were chosen and of what?
☐ What were the differences (if any) in the sort of pictures chosen by each group?
☐ How did the presenter seek to capture his or her audience's interest?

PART 2 Take *one* of the gospel stories below and distribute it to all the groups. Their task is the same as before, but they have not only to convey the original story but also how it relates to today.

☐ Peter's denial   Mark 14:66-72
☐ The transfiguration   Matthew 17:1-13
☐ Jesus' baptism   John 1:29-42

When the group reassembles, ask the same questions as in part 1. Pay particular attention to the last question: how did the presenter make the story gripping? You may also find it interesting to discuss how their presentations differ from a typical sermon on the same passage!

What's Your World View?

Are you wearing glasses to read this? If they fit well and are the right strength, then for most of the time you probably forget you have got them on. You're so used to seeing the world through them that you take them for granted.

But it only takes a scratch on one lens (or a bike ride on a wet day) for a complete change of view. Suddenly you're uncomfortably aware of how much you depend on them. Most wearers of glasses would agree that the only time you start to notice your specs is when something goes wrong with them.

The vision thing

Even if you are fortunate enough to have perfect vision, there is still a sense in which you, too, are wearing specs. We all need to make sense of the world around us and, without some kind of lens to bring the picture into focus, our experience of life is going to be a confusing blur.

The lens we are looking through is our *world view:* the assumptions, beliefs and priorities that put life into perspective. It's the *way* we interpret life, not life itself — and most of the time we're not even aware that we have a world view. In fact, when we are, we simply call it common sense.

The word 'common' is important because every community is based on *shared* assumptions. Our ideas of good and evil, right and wrong, justice and injustice are communal, not individual. A world view isn't a personal thing. It's the basis of a culture.

So a world view is rather like a pair of optical lenses through which we're all looking at life. And I'm going to suggest that the way the world is changing means that we're urgently in need of a visit to the optician.

But first let's investigate our current prescription.

'The lens we are looking through is our world view.'

The meaning of life

Most of our ideas about the meaning of life aren't as old as we think. They date back some 250 years to the so-called 'Age of Reason' when much of our modern way of thinking emerged. What we see as common sense has not always seemed so, and not all of it has proved to be good sense.

9

What have been the basic assumptions of our Western world view?

☐ *We (not God) are in charge.* We live in a scientific age created by our own ability to think rationally, and we're increasingly able to understand what makes our world tick. By the clever application of our intelligence and skill we've conquered many diseases and put a man on the moon. So it's not surprising that...

☐ *We believe in progress.* We are on the way to a better and better world. In much of the world, science and technology really have delivered a better way of life. And we have come to expect an ever increasing standard of living. The scientific approach seems to have paid dividends and therefore...

> 66 Western culture... is rooted in an underlying and unifying world view. That world view, like all world views, tells a story. The Western story is the myth of progress. 99
> Brian Walsh *Subversive Christianity*

☐ *We value objectivity.* Seeing is believing. We claim to believe only what we can work out and 'prove' for ourselves. And so we're very selective about what we allow into the arena of public life. Then, because there are some things which can't be subjected to scientific tests, we've come to believe that...

☐ *Religion is a matter of private opinion.* We assume there's a difference between matters of fact and matters of faith. Facts can be proved, faith can't. Questions about the purpose of life are matters of faith. And we're happy to tolerate a wide spectrum of faith because...

☐ *We believe that to be truly human individuals have to have every possible freedom.* So during the last 200 years we've abolished slavery and are attempting to guarantee basic human rights. We are working for a society of maximum freedom and maximum tolerance. And we see no reason why we can't succeed because...

☐ *We believe people are basically good.* All they need is a good education and soon we will have a society where right and wrong are obvious to everyone.

Nothing succeeds like success

The Age of Reason gave us a very practical world view. With it we have transformed the world out of all recognition. Life is infinitely better than it was. None of us would want to go back to a pre-scientific age.

> 66 The super-industrial revolution can erase hunger, disease, ignorance and brutality.
> Alvin Toffler *Future Shock* 99

But our success has bred confidence, arrogance even. Our world view convinced us that, given time, there was no problem that we couldn't crack. And, on the whole, our track record has been excellent.

Experience versus explanation
But check that list again.

Isn't it hopelessly optimistic? Are all problems automatically solvable by human ingenuity? Has the twentieth century delivered all that we hoped?

Whether I'm talking to university professors or people on the street, I detect a conflict between what we've taken for granted about life in the past and what we are actually experiencing now.

Few people now believe that we are on an automatic path to a better world. For many the dream of progress has been replaced by hopelessness. When Bishop Leslie Newbigin came back from India after more than 30 years as a missionary, he said the hardest thing he had to face was 'the disappearance of hope'.

---

66 There is little sign among the citizens of this country of the sort of confidence in the future which was certainly present in the earlier years of this century. 99
Leslie Newbigin *The Other Side of 1984*

Instead we are in a time of crisis.

Our way of life has been destroying the environment. The ozone layer and the rain forests have become subjects of general concern. And if we are not recycling, our children will want to know why!

Science may have worked wonders but it has also created the possibility of nuclear destruction.

Instead of a 'new world order' there is an increase of violent nationalism.

Aids seems to resist all attempts to find a cure and yet there is little serious commitment to change our sexual lifestyles.

We have moved from a belief in objective truth to a time when no one seems sure of anything beyond what they feel.

Our individualism has lead to the breakdown of community and family. 'There is no such thing as society,' we were told. We wanted to be free from restraint rather than free to serve, and now we don't know how to sustain life together.

Our experience makes a nonsense of the old explanations. The old glasses don't fit any more. In fact they have become part of our problem. Check the list again. What makes up the prescription?

ACID RAIN OF THE SPIRIT

Consider the growing alarm about acid rain. Borne on the shifting winds of expanding industrialisation, acid rain is becoming a problem of planetary dimensions. A leisurely but lethal atmospheric plague, it brings its silent devastation not only to lakes, forests and wildlife but to the world's great buildings and statues.

'Secularisation' is the acid rain of the spirit, the atmospheric cancer of the mind and the imagination. Vented into the air not only by industrial chimneys but by computer terminals, marketing techniques and management insights, it is washed down in the rain, shower by shower, the deadliest destroyer of religious life the world has ever seen.

By secularisation, I mean the process through which, starting from the centre and moving outwards, successive sectors of society and culture have been freed from the decisive influence of religious ideas and institutions.

Consider for a moment what was involved in the Apollo moon landing in 1969. No operation could be more characteristically modern, yet it was really no different in principle from designing a car or marketing a perfume. Strip away the awesomeness of the vision and the pride of achievement, and what remains? A vast assembly of plans and procedures, all carefully calculated and minutely controlled in which nothing is left to chance. By the same token, nothing is left to human spontaneity or divine intervention.

Medieval Christians could have as their maxim, 'I dress their wounds, but God heals them.' But how many modern Christians doing agricultural service in Africa would think of saying, 'I irrigated the desert, but God made it grow'? The problem for the Christian in the modern world is not that practical reason is irreligious, but that in more and more areas of life religion is practically irrelevant. Total indifference to religion is characteristic of the central and expanding areas of modern life. The deadly rain has fallen and all the spiritual life in its path is dead, stunted or deformed.

Os Guinness *The Gravedigger File,* Hodder and Stoughton 1983

Facts set against faith; a lot about cause and effect, nothing about purpose; masses about the individual, nothing about community; all about the human race, nothing about God. Some areas can be seen in pin-sharp focus, while others have been cut out completely.

66 We are nearing the end of a period in human civilization in which there seemed to be no limits to individual choice and collective progress. 99
Rabbi Jonathan Sachs *The Persistence of Faith*

Requiem for a culture?

Our glasses are hurting our eyes. When it comes to evaluating our situation at the end of the century, our human-centred world view just isn't up to the job. The old assumptions and explanations seem well past their sell-by date.

I believe that we're living in a time of culture shift. Our world view no longer seems viable for a very simple reason — the culture that it shaped is dying. Its weaknesses have brought it to its end.

66 Cultures are born and die. The question now is whether we are at a time when a culture is approaching death. 99
Leslie Newbigin *The Other Side of 1984*

We're living at a time when most people are more sure what they don't believe than what they do. So it is hardly surprising that we are uncertain about the shape of the future. But whatever emerges we are going to need a new pair of glasses, a new world view.

Men and women are hungry for answers in a culture that has run out of them. For the Church that has to be an amazing opportunity.

Explaining the Bible Today

**AIM** *To look at how the New Testament draws on the culture of its day to explain vital truths about God and our relationship with him.*

_____

EXERCISE 1 *To all the saints at Philippi*

Some would claim that Jesus told simple stories to impart spiritual truths, but believe that his followers, such as the apostle Paul, preached nothing but complicated doctrine.

Split the group into three and ask all the sub-groups to skim through the whole of Paul's letter to the Philippians.

☐ Group 1 should note any 'pictures' Paul paints to describe his beliefs and teaching. For example, he says the Philippians 'shine like stars in the universe' (2:15).

☐ Group 2 should note references to Paul's own life and experiences. How does he relate Christian teaching to his own life? What is Paul's story of faith?

☐ Group 3 should note the half dozen or so key teaching points and jot these down as simple phrases. For example, in chapter 2 Paul says that we must imitate Christ's humility.

Allow, at most, 15 minutes for this exercise. Bring the small groups together and exchange lists. Start with group 3, perhaps listing the teaching points on an overhead projector. From the other two groups see how Paul illuminates his teaching by colourful analogies and his own experiences.

_____

EXERCISE 2 *Why Jesus died*

The apostles looked to aspects of their world to use as descriptions for what Christ has done on the cross. So Paul, for example, talked in terms of our freedom from slavery and being declared not guilty in a court of law.

Photocopy the page (opposite) of statements of why Jesus died. Ask people in the group to consider which they feel says most to them. You could ask people to ring their first choice.

We, too, need to explain the gospel based on every-day sights and experiences. Where in *our* culture is there hostility and a breakdown in communication? How can we use these examples as starting points to express our separation from God without Christ? (An example could be marriage breakdown and reconciliation.)

Explain that analogies or pictures only express part of the truth. If pushed too far, they can be misleading. For example, marriage breakdown and reconciliation may express separation and forgiveness, but usually both parties are at fault. With God, it is only we who are to blame.

Why Jesus Died

Buying and selling

The slave market was a common sight in the ancient world. We are slaves to sin yet we cannot buy our way out. Jesus has bought us back; he has redeemed us.

'In him (Jesus) we have redemption through his own blood, the forgiveness of our sins.' Ephesians 1:7

Not guilty!

Breaking laws makes a person guilty in a court of law. The consequence or punishment for sin is death. Jesus has died for us yet we can be acquitted and treated as innocent.

'Since we have been justified through faith, we have peace with God.' Romans 5:1

Well-known stories

Every culture has its set of well-known stories. Jesus and the apostles often referred back to the Old Testament.

'Just as Moses lifted up the snake in the desert, so the Son of Man must be lifted up.' John 3:14

Part of the family

Roman society was used to adoption. Under Roman law an adopted son had all the privileges of a natural son.

'God sent forth his son... to redeem those who were under the law, so that we might receive adoption as sons.' Galatians 4:4-5

Triumph

Whenever the victorious Roman army returned home there was a triumphal procession, with the defeated prisoners paraded for ridicule. Jesus has defeated the power of death and the time will come when his victory will be fully and publicly seen.

'Having disarmed the powers and authorities, Christ makes a public spectacle of them, triumphing over them by the cross.' Colossians 2:15

Broken relationships

Through our own fault we can easily fall out with our friends. We have turned our back on God's friendship and need to be reconciled to him.

'If anyone is in Christ, he is a new creation.... All this is from God, who through Christ reconciled us to himself.' 2 Corinthians 5:17-18

Sacrifice

In the Old Testament the life-blood of animals was shed for sin. These sacrifices looked forward to the death of Jesus that deals effectively with our guilt before God.

'God presented him (Jesus) as a sacrifice of atonement.' Romans 3:25

Polishing our Glasses

To discover our world view: the glasses through which we and others view the world.

PART 1 To start the group thinking about what people outside the church believe, ask them to guess which magazines are the most popular and why? Some circulation figures for magazines are given here.

What sections of these magazines are likely to be the most read? What does this say about what people find important and interesting?

She magazine has on its cover, 'For women who juggle their lives'. *Chic* has, 'The lifestyle magazine for women who can choose' and *Top Santé* says, 'The magazine about feeling and looking good'. Split the group up into twos and threes and ask these groups to come up with a slogan that for them captures what is important for one of:

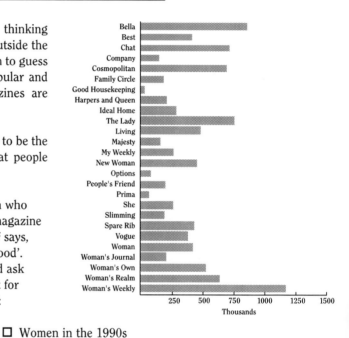

☐ Men in the 1990s   ☐ Women in the 1990s
☐ Teenagers in the 1990s   ☐ Elderly people in the 1990s

PART 2 What do people who seldom, if ever, come to church believe? Write each key word below on to an overhead projector or write it out on a large sheet of paper that can be pinned up, asking for responses as you go. Ask people to shout out what they know are some of the common beliefs about the word. Encourage them to think of their non-Christian friends and colleagues. Before you move on to the next word, ask the group to say which of the responses are most common among their friends.

God	*Purpose in life*	*Sin*	*Destiny*
Freedom	*Acceptance*	*Jesus*	*Christian*

PART 3 If you are working through this book with a group, you may find it helpful to revisit Part 2 and look at how a Christian would react to the same words. Where are the differences? And is there a way we can communicate what we believe in a way which will make sense? You may want to take one word such as *destiny* and work through how a Christian can explain his or her beliefs.

Pick 'n' Mix at the Pluralist Superstore

If ours is a multi-cultural, multi-choice society, then our leading '-ism' has to be pluralism. And it comes in two varieties.

Pluralism mark 1

Pluralism – mark 1 – is the stage of realizing that ours is just one among many world views. All the other major faiths have their own particular 'prescription lenses' to help them make sense of life. And, of course, secular society offers its own selection of specs: examine them and you'll probably discover the brand names Marx or Freud.

It's a situation that is as old as the Church itself. The early Christians lived lives of radical challenge to the prevailing world views of their day.

They, like us, knew that their faith was seen as one among many competing truth-claims. Given sufficient information, men and women had to decide which one to choose.

But this is not our present situation.

Pluralism mark 2

In all of us there is a deep need to make sense of the world. Even in a 'permanent present' the questions beneath the surface won't go away. Men and women continue to feel a powerful, if unfocused, yearning for meaning.

But the search for meaning is no longer a matter of the mark 1 'Department store' approach of choosing between self-contained truth-claims. In the Department store you buy (unless you are rich!) one suit or one skirt from the many on display. So pluralism mark 1 is about choosing one religion or world view from the many on offer. But we've left all that behind. Today we prefer the pick 'n'mix counter.

Choice is what matters. People today make up their own prescription for their glasses. Bombarded with images and alternatives they see no reason to accept one off-the-shelf world view rather than another. They customize. Like children at the sweet counter, they pick and mix ideas and experiences that feel good or seem to make sense. It's a DIY world view.

---

66 Pluralism, the 'ism' of our time, has become the great problem and the great opportunity. 99
Charles Jencks *What is Post-Modernism?*

Some pick 'n' mix ingredients are traditional: we select some bits of folk Christianity or beliefs about right and wrong, maybe some things our family has always thought. But because we are rootless, we have forgotten how they used to fit into a wider framework. We may still believe them without knowing why they are true. Other ingredients will come from other cultures and religions, from TV soaps, astrologers, pop stars and agony aunts — all pulled together to make some sense.

Chat to a young person and you may be delighted to find a very positive attitude to Jesus. But probe a little deeper and you may discover your friend has an equally strong belief in re-incarnation or spirit guides. He or she feels no tension between the different ingredients of their own spiritual 'special selection'.

We're living in a time when it's easy to believe two impossible contradictory things, not just before breakfast, but simultaneously.

The New Age remix

The New Age Movement is an important example of pick and mix pluralism.

☐ It provides clear evidence of the renewal of interest in spiritual experience.
It claims to answer a number of vital concerns: the future of the planet, where people fit into the universe, the search for wholeness, a basis for hope, and viable alternatives to the blinkers of both the 'Age of Reason' and the 'perpetual present'.

☐ It offers new glasses: a world view fluid enough for a pluralist society but coherent enough to form the basis of many networks. And it is created by pick and mix.

In pop music terms it is a remix. It's no more than samples of ancient and modern sources mixed together in new combinations. New Age thinking draws from Eastern religion (Hinduism especially), from tribal religions, pre-Christian paganism and nature worship. It simultaneously samples forms of spiritualism, astrology and the occult, environmental theories, psychology and the new physics. It distrusts much of Western science and technology and has a major interest in alternative remedies and therapies.

The chief framework of the world view is drawn from Hinduism (God is everything and everything is one, reincarnation, karma and so on) but with two important distinctions. Concern for the planet makes New Agers world affirming rather than world denying — and little interest is shown in more self-denying forms of spiritual discipline.

---

66 The New Age movement is better viewed as a world-view shift than a unified global conspiracy. **99**
Douglas Groothuis *Unmasking the New Age*

New Age is not a conspiracy but an extensive network or networks of people with overlapping concerns and convictions. Many people today share some of the convictions without being part of any movement. This whole thing is evidence of a big swing in Western thinking. In fact, despite the Eastern sources, it is a very Western movement. It is like a religion without being a religion. It is not concerned so much with God as with self fulfilment, and it recognizes no moral absolutes.

New Age followers share some concerns and convictions with Christians. They share a belief in the spiritual realm and a sense of responsibility for the environment, among others. Some of them live exemplary lives. But the world view itself is profoundly opposed to Christian teaching for it denies the existence of a personal creator, the uniqueness of Christ, the reality of sin and the need of atonement. The issues being faced are critical for our future, but the glasses are dark, blotting out the parts of reality that don't fit.

Pick your own

The New Age movement is classic pick 'n'mix. A little pre-Christian religion, a few distorted bits of accepted creeds, some new physics and a dash of popular psychology: stir together and sprinkle with any extra 'alternatives' you might fancy.

All that's needed next is to find some people who have picked and mixed in more or less the same way and you've got yourself a community.

A matter of choice

What are the implications for Christians as they seek to share their faith?

When my choice is what matters, I'm likely to be suspicious of anyone who seems to threaten that choice. We have become deeply wary of those in authority. We want a change of political leaders but don't intend to trust them. More than that, we're unwilling to trust those who claim to have explanations about the whole of life. What right have they to tell me how to live?

Here we have a problem. Christ claims to be 'the way, the truth and the life' and the early church

preached that 'there is no other name under heaven by which we may be saved.' How can we present such demanding, absolute claims to friends who will see us as playing power games? We may recommend soap powders, films and even a trip to Disney Land, but we dare not claim to believe absolute truth. The only absolute these days is to say there is no absolute.

Power and weakness

It's a harsh climate for evangelism. Your motivation may be a simple longing to tell your friends about God's love. But that's not how it's interpreted.

As long as you keep your self-selected spirituality to yourself, there's no problem. Try and share it and it's seen as an attempt to impose.

Our Church of England is seen as a hierarchical, male dominated, historic institution: all the things our culture finds increasingly difficult to accept. It is vital we treat these suspicions seriously for the power of God is demonstrated in human weakness, not in archaic, defensive institutions.

Words and pictures

We also face another challenge. And again it is one that the Church is not well equipped to address. Our culture is image-based. Pictures matter more than words. Our knowledge of the world comes to us in thousands of image-fragments and behind each picture is a story.

19

Faith, hope... but not too much clarity

Religion has been reduced to the level of just one or more consumer choice. Ours is the age of the DIY god, where you make your deity to fit your lifestyle. It would have parallels with the idol worship of ancient cultures were it not for the fact that the worshipper always remains firmly in control of the deity, adapting it at the slightest hint that it might interfere inconveniently with his or her lifestyle.

Take a bit of Buddhism, perhaps a hint of pantheism, get yourself centred, add a smidgen of self-help philosophy, a drop of astrology and perhaps a small spoon of Christianity – but nothing doctrinaire – and you have made your own faith. Authority is out, experience is in. You do not need to go to a church, synagogue or mosque and you will not need to adhere to a clearly defined set of moral teachings – with the odd exception.

Dr Grace Davie at the department of Sociology at Exeter University says that,

while the incidence of religious practice has declined in Britain, this has not been accompanied by a decline in religious belief. People have detached practice from belief, which has led to 'a substantial block of undirected spirituality'.

Perhaps it is a reaction to eighties materialism, perhaps it is because the end is always nigh with a millennium, but if Europeans are detaching themselves from traditional religions, they are not abandoning religious faith. People are essentially faith-full, wherever they are, whatever their culture. The question is what they put their faith in.

'We do not live in a secular society,' says Davie, 'We live in a society in which belief is drifting away from the orthodoxy to no one knows where; in which belief is floating, disconnected without an anchor.'

Martin Wroe in *The Observer*, December 1993

I think this is the key to understanding how people now learn. People build up a mosaic of small, vivid images. If we are serious about reaching them we need to realize that there's a generation for whom connected abstract argument is a non-starter. If words are being used then they've got to be words that create pictures in the mind.

However, much of what we've learnt about explaining the gospel has not followed this approach. We may talk of the yawning gap between us and God — and that Christ can bridge that gap — but we quickly overlay this simple picture with an 'A then B then C then D' explanation of what God has done for us in Christ. We're so concerned to explain gospel concepts that we miss out on the biggest picture available to us all: the story of our own Christian lives and what Christ has done (and is doing) for us.

66 We live in an age where the visual seems to have taken over from the verbal. 99
Robert Hewison *Future Tense*

In our church services we rely on the spoken word and on service books of innumerable pages. The sermon is in a form that non-Christians find difficult to relate to. Even the most serious news item on the TV is presented in five minutes and is based around the story of an individual. Gas bill increases are focused through the example of a pensioner, war atrocities through the story of a bereaved woman or a harassed hospital doctor.

Stories and images have replaced argument and discourse.

'We rely on service books of innumerable pages.'

This does not mean that people are less rational, simply that they get their information in a new, more fragmented way. They still piece it all together to create something meaningful.

Maybe we need to go back to Jesus to rediscover how to convey truth in a non-book culture: in meaningful parable and gripping story.

Challenge to change

New ways of seeing, hearing and learning. A world where the power to choose is all important. A world which says: 'You are on your journey. I'm on mine. Let's respect each other's choice — after all they're both equally valid.' In a multi-choice society the claims of the gospel are bound to cause offence.

Of course the content of our message must remain constant. But we need to re-evaluate the ways in which we try to communicate the truth. We've got to find new ways of telling our story that will help our friends and neighbours to stop, listen and understand.

21

CPAS © 1994

The early church faced a similar challenge. Jesus was a Jew preaching mainly to Jews, but his gospel was intended for the whole world. God used a Paul, raised in both Jewish and Greek/Roman cultures, to take it to the wider world. Jesus spoke of 'the kingdom of God', taught in parables drawn from Palestinian rural life, and demonstrated that God was a forgiving God by sharing meals with social outcasts. Paul too spoke of God's forgiveness but he expressed it in terms of the Roman law courts (justification), Roman slavery (redemption) and Roman child adoption. He debated in public, sometimes quoted local poets and philosophers, and wrote long letters. His choice of words and methods came from his culture. Yet the message was the same.

The same challenge has occurred every time there is a new missionary opportunity. We call it 'cross-cultural mission'. We understand that when someone goes to serve Christ in another country they have to learn the language and the culture to be able to communicate the gospel there. It is just the same when there is a culture shift of the kind I am describing. Only it is far harder to recognize it in our own backyard because culture shifts happen so gradually.

> **❝** We are caught between two ages, one passing, the other not yet born. **❞**
> Rabbi Jonathan Sachs *The Persistence of Faith*

To some degree all of us are living in two cultures. The old one hasn't completely died and the new one hasn't taken full shape yet. Some of our old ways of evangelism will still work with some people, but many others will require a new approach. Again Paul can help us. He did his evangelism in two different cultures: Jewish and Greek/Roman. Each required an approach that was culturally relevant. 'To the Jews I became as a Jew in order to win Jews..., to those outside the law... [Greeks and Romans] I became as one outside the law so that I might win those outside the law. I do it all for the sake of the gospel.' (See 1 Corinthians: 9:19-23.)

In the same way we must learn to express the gospel of eternity in the medium of today.

Religion on the Menu

AIM *To help the group to see that many of the choices we make are purely matters of personal taste, and that non-believers often see religious beliefs in these terms.*

PART 1 Explain that the group is to open, together, a new pub or restaurant. Ask each person to think of their ideal pub or restaurant meal. Which starter, main dish and sweet would each person choose? Put them into small groups and ask each group to present its agreed meal as part of the overall menu. (The group will know that the choice of dishes is largely a matter of taste: steak and kidney is no 'better' than gammon or curry.)

PART 2 Write up the list of beliefs below (or photocopy the bottom half of this page) and ask the group together to pick out the beliefs their neighbours and colleagues at work hold. Add others not mentioned. Which beliefs are more common than others?

☐ Ask the group which six, and then which three, beliefs Christians might choose.

☐ How do they feel handling religious beliefs much as they handled the selection of meals for a menu?

It's asking for trouble to do something on Friday 13th.
You need to stick by your mates
There is no heaven and hell, only re-incarnation
Happiness is what it's all about
Love your neighbour as yourself
Our lives are destined
There's no God
There's only one true God: all other religions are half-truths
Horoscopes provide a guide to our personality and events
Continuing the family line is important
God is a personal creator
Freedom comes through abandoning religion as an emotional crutch
We should focus on the here and now, not the hereafter
We'll all get to heaven if we're good
Jesus died for my sin and rose again
All religions lead to God
Scientific explanations rule out the need for God
We're one with the universe, one with Nature
It doesn't matter what you believe
It's all right as long as you don't harm others

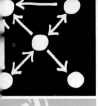

Don't Tell Me What to Believe!

AIM

To help the group to see the difference between 'public facts and private values' and how this affects our evangelism.

EXERCISE

There are 'facts' which we feel everyone should agree with: '2 + 2 = 4' and 'the sun rises in the East'. Then there are values which we leave to each person's choice: 'I think capital punishment is wrong'. We tend to regard scientific statements as 'facts' (and therefore entirely trustworthy) but religious and moral views as more a matter of personal belief.

If there is one God, revealed in Jesus Christ, is not this as much a matter of fact as 'Helium is an inert gas'? But because religion is now seen as a matter of personal values, people no longer look for 'truth' but only what works or is helpful *for them*.

Write the statements below on an overhead projector. Ask the group to imagine they are wandering though their local secondary school, eavesdropping on the lessons and discussions taking place. They hear the statements, but which are *facts* to which everyone agrees and which are just *opinions*? Over which statements might they and non-Christian friends differ?

☐ There are public facts and private opinions. Is science *always* in the 'facts' group?

☐ Why is religion for many a matter of their own private opinions and what difference does this make to our presentation of what we see as the truth?

☐ Look at Acts 3 - 4:22. The apostle Peter talked of people acting in 'ignorance' (3:17) and there being salvation in 'no other name' (4:12). Where are the difficulties in speaking like this today?

Maths:	*'2 + 2 = 4'*
Religious Education:	*'All religions form equal ways to God'*
History:	*'Henry VIII was a good king'*
Chemistry:	*'Helium is an inert gas'*
Political studies:	*'At least fascism in Italy made the railways run on time'*
Economics:	*'Monetarism simply does not work'*
Playground:	*'Miss Pringle is really horrible'*
Physics:	*'Light is a stream of tiny particles'*
Home economics:	*'Fat is bad for the arteries'*
Biology:	*'Darwin's beliefs on evolution are now known to be true'*
Christian Union:	*'Jesus is the Way the Truth and the Life'*
Personal development:	*'Sex is OK provided it's within a loving relationship'*

Telling Your Story

Culture shifts, a revolution in ways of thinking and learning..., it's enough to discourage anybody from sharing their faith. But we don't need to be defeatist. There *is* something we can do.

But it's not this way: 'Here are the facts that I believe – if you want to become a Christian you must believe them too. Now let me explain them to you....'

Good intentions, certainly. And you may have an excellent step-by-step presentation of the gospel. But is this kind of 'logical progression' approach really appropriate for today's image generation? I don't think so.

Following my guide
Here are some things you might try saying instead.

☐ *'May I share my story with you – of what Jesus has done for me?'* (See 1 John 1:1-4.)

By saying this you're offering a personal narrative, not a formula. But implicit in your story is a confrontation with an unpalatable idea that Jesus is Lord of all and that he calls all to follow him.

Of course, I'm not suggesting we abandon the kind of public proclamation that is bound to contain an element of 'take it or leave it'. I'm talking about starting points.

☐ *'I've found the one I believe to be the true guide.'* (See John 14:6 and Hebrews 12:2.)

This is a simple statement, but it has profound implications. You're saying, 'Contrary to our culture, I really believe he's the guide for *all* people.'

Then take the opportunity to talk about the claims of Christ. There is no one so attractive as Jesus, and a relationship with him is the heart of our message.

☐ *'I still have a lot to learn.'* (See Philippians 3:12-14.)

' *"We've got it, you haven't - so shape up!"* '

'I'm learning to follow him and I've found him totally faithful. There's loads I've yet to learn, but why don't you come with me and learn from him with me.' This is a personal, very humble approach. It's non-threatening and a million miles from the arrogance of, 'Here are the facts. We've got it, you haven't – so shape up.'

☐ *'We travel together and we learn from one another.'* (See Romans 12:5 and Ephesians 3:18-19.)

Beginning with the story of your own journey is important because you'll be sharing that it's a journey that can't be made alone: when you meet the guide you meet the others who follow him. You're saying, 'We've found a way to be a community again.'

CHAPTER FOUR

☐ *'We've got roots.'* (See Hebrews 2:1.)

We claim to know where we come from. Stretching back behind us are generations of men and women who've proved the guide to be true. Their story helps and encourages us today.

☐ *'We know where we're going.'* (See Philippians 1:23 and 2 Timothy 4:7-8.)

This isn't a journey for its own sake. Because of Jesus' resurrection, Christians are people of hope. We know that death is not the end and that there is a future for the earth.

☐ *'There is a cost.'* (See 1 Peter 2:9-12, 21-25.)

There was a cost born by Jesus who died to forgive us and make it possible for us to set out on this journey and complete it safely. There is a cost to our pride in recognizing we need help and forgiveness.

There's no need to pretend that your story is pain-free. Following our guide is no picnic — sometimes it feels as if we're trudging through alien territory. But you can add, 'Yes, it is tough but I'm absolutely confident about my destination.'

Pointing to Jesus

In all this you're saying some amazing things: 'I'm

rooted in the *past*. I've a clear vision for the *future*. I've something to offer in terms of *community*.'

Have you noticed what's happening? In telling your story you are actually providing answers to the basic questions of a crumbling culture. And all the time you are pointing to Jesus.

Linking to the earth's story

Evangelism must relate to the great issues of the day. A new attitude to the environment must be part of any future world view. On that subject the Bible has a lot to say.

For conversation with the growing number of people who are deeply concerned about the future of the planet, why not try the approach oulined below?

If you see the relevance of this part of the Bible's teaching today, check it out against your own life first. You can't use the environment as an excuse to talk about Jesus. You have to care about it because he does.

☐ *Begin at the end*
Rather than starting with your experience of Jesus, which seems an irrelevance compared with the destruction of the planet, start with the Christian hope for a new (meaning 'renewed') heaven

and earth. Look at Isaiah 65:17-25, 2 Peter 3:8-13 and Revelation 21:1-7. In all these passages 'new' means restored, not today's demand to throw it away and start again.

---

66 God is preparing for the birth of a new creation a new heaven and a new earth.... The creator God is at work within history to bring forth a future in which all things will be made new. For whatever reason the creator invites us to participate as collaborators in birthing this new order in our lives, in our communities and in the wider world. 99
Tom Sine *Wild Hope*

We Christians are sure that God has guaranteed a future for the earth. One day he will make it new. We care about the earth because God cares. We humans are directly responsible for much of the damage that has been done, and Christians are called to be part of God's answer now.

☐ *The end has already begun*
The resurrection of Jesus is the start and the guarantee of the new creation. His risen body – the same but different – is a picture of our future and the earth's future. He gives us hope, and his power is available to help us change the way we live. If he did not rise, we might as well just live for now because now is all we can be sure of (1 Corinthians 15).

☐ *The new world begins at home*
There's no point campaigning for 'green' issues if we're not prepared to change our own lifestyles. Christians believe we need Christ's power to do that. We haven't so much wronged the earth as the one who made it. For the earth's sake and our own, we need to get right with him. That is what Jesus made possible by dying and rising for us. A Christian is a 'new creation' – someone who has a part in God's future world *and* who can work towards it now (2 Corinthians 5:17-21, Romans 5:17).

---

66 There is... a God shaped hole in our ozone layer. 99
Rabbi Jonathan Sachs *The Persistence of Faith*

☐ *Childbirth not terminal illness*
Christians are meant to be the source of hope for the planet. Because our bodies still get sick and die, and because we know we are often unlike Jesus, we can identify with the pain, frustration and decay of our world, because we are still part of it. But because of our relationship to Jesus, we don't lose hope – we know the future. The pains are labour pains. They are real and very painful, but they offer the possibility of new life for the world. Through Jesus we even feel God's pain over our broken world. We care because he cares. And on his behalf we offer hope (Romans 8:18-27).

Lost for Words

Telling our own story of faith is very powerful. People are used to hearing stories and will be able to identify with our experience. TV soaps are more popular than documentaries, and a simple, yet personal, testimony can be more effective than endless well-argued sermons!

Clear structure

It is vital that your story has a clear structure. There are a number of possible examples for this.

Example 1: *Before, during, after*
What I was like *before* I became a Christian.
What Christ did for me and how I responded.
What difference it has made.

Example 2: *Realize, react, result*
When I *realized* God was at work in my life.
How I *reacted* to what God had done for me.
The *result* of what has happened.

Example 3: *Called, challenged, changed*
God *called* me.
God *challenged* me.
God has *changed* me.

Examples one and two more readily lend themselves to the person who has had a definite time when they were not a Christian. Example three is particularly good for the person who has always grown up knowing God's love and can remember significant steps along the way of growing into an adult relationship with God (for example, the time when you first understood what Jesus had done on the cross for you, an occasion when a doubt or difficulty was dealt with).

Once you have chosen a structure, work with it until you have it well established in your mind. As a guide, half of your story should focus on what Jesus has done for you and how you responded.

———

Key question 1: 'Will this make *sense* for the person who isn't a Christian?'

———

Focus on God

The great danger of telling our story is we so often focus on ourselves that we forget God is at the heart of our story. He is the one who called us to himself; without his initiative we would not be Christians!

How do we focus on God without preaching? Simply by ensuring we tell *our* story and don't try to persuade them it should be *their* story. The language should be 'I' and 'me', not 'you'.

———

Key question 2: 'Does this help the person to discover good news about *Jesus*?'

———

Learn from St Paul

Paul was converted in a dramatic way and was not shy in telling his story. His conversion is recorded in Acts 9, and Luke (the author of Acts) recounts how Paul retold it in Acts 22:4-16 and Acts 26:9-18. Paul also gave an much-abbreviated version to the Galatians: Galatians 1:13-17.

Avoid jargon

The following are unlikely to be helpful elements of your story:

☐ Jargon   ☐ Exaggeration

☐ Too much content   ☐ Repetition

☐ Irrelevance   ☐ Hidden assumptions

☐ Arrogance   ☐ Being critical

One way to avoid these elements is to ask a Christian friend to listen to your story; another way is to ask a non-Christian friend to listen and comment! As a last resort, use a cassette recorder and play it back to yourself.

Practise

The following may help us to refine the way we tell our story. The better we know it the more confident we will be, the more we can listen to the person, the more flexible our approach,

☐ Write it out in full and try it out on a friend.

☐ Link your story with something the person says.

☐ Illustrate it from daily life.

☐ Ask questions of the person about their experience.

☐ Be gentle and humble, use humour if possible.

☐ Practise it often.

Pray

Pray for opportunities to tell your story.

'People are used to hearing stories.'

☐ *When time runs out*

Many people are aware that we have only so much time to halt the destruction of our environment. They also know that not everyone has the will to change their attitude or lifestyle. However little or much we achieve, Christians believe that only God can restore the earth. And when he does it he will judge each human being, for humans are stewards of creation. Everything was created through and for Jesus. Failed stewards need to find forgiveness and a new commission from him, for one day time will run out (Colossians 1:15-20, Revelation 20:11-21:4).

Factors leading to faith

It is easy to believe that what our friends need is the latest evangelistic book or a 10-round bout with a powerful evangelist. But it's not true.

John Finney, as the Church of England's Officer for the Decade of Evangelism, set out at the start of the Decade to discover what led people to faith. His book *Finding Faith Today* makes fascinating reading. He was well aware that the most important factor in people becoming Christians was the work of the Holy Spirit. But he wanted to discover what hindered or helped the Spirit's work.

Those in the survey were first asked what they considered to be the main factor which led them to become a Christian, or a more committed Christian. They were given a wide range of possibilities ranging from parental influence to Christian books.

As the main factor in the journey to faith and in helping along the way, *friends* rated very highly indeed — the figures were not far behind the influence of the family. They far exceeded the effect of literature or sermons. Friends gave love, care, understanding and prayers. And the combination was powerful.

He also asked participants if they regarded one special person as particularly influential or whether it was a group of people. Only about a quarter looked to one person as the key influence though, of course, there may have been one person who had been particularly helpful or who had introduced them to the group. His research showed that to belong to a group of friends who were Christians was important.

He concluded that friendship needs time and that churches should not demand so much commitment to activities and meetings that families and friends are neglected. Having no time to make new friends means little chance of effective evangelism.

──────────

66 For most people the corporate life of the church is a vital element in the process of becoming a Christian and for about a quarter it is the vital factor. **99**

John Finney *Finding Faith Today*

──────────

CPAS © 1994

Only one person in four in Britain today has any sort of grasp of the main content of what Christians believe. This is likely to shrink further as only one is seven children is in regular touch with a church. It has also been shown that new people are only likely to stay in church if they make six or seven potential new friends in the first six months. Put all this together and it is clear that for many people their journey into faith needs to *begin* through the witness of a Christian friend and *continue* in some form of 'Just Looking' or 'Christian Foundations' group in which they can make friends at the same time as asking questions and learning about faith.

We don't always have to wait for events like these. As well as natural opportunities to share our experience of Jesus, it is often right to offer to pray for or with a friend in a time of stress or sickness. Answers to prayers demand an explanation too!

Experience to explanation

Our culture makes barriers against the gospel. Getting across the divide is difficult. I'm suggesting that there's a very simple way across — straightforward, carefully thought-through personal testimony.

So am I saying that reason is out of date? Have we said goodbye to the days of laying our cards on the table in a sensible sequence?

Absolutely not. We still need to be able to make a rational, ordered case for our faith, and a small group is an ideal place to do that. But we need to understand the value of an evangelism that begins where people are.

Previously we were used to presenting the facts of the gospel in a reasoned way and inviting people to respond so that they would know Christ for themselves. We moved from *explanation to experience*. Today we will often need to work from *experience to explanation*.

And it's to our advantage that spiritual experience is something that is increasingly acceptable in our multi-choice society. Many people will acknowledge experiences which they would label as spiritual or profound: a sense of a greater presence during a time of crisis, or of being carried through a bereavement. Of course, for many people it's also very hard to put such feelings into words — particularly, in our culture, if you're a man.

***

66 Twenty years ago it seemed as if religion had run its course in the modern world. Today a more considered view would be that its story has hardly yet begun. 99

Robin Gill *Moral Communities*

***

What matters is that we don't dismiss such 'encounters' because they aren't specifically Christian — nor should we treat them as 'occult' unless we have specific reasons. It is the work of the Holy Spirit to make people aware of the spiritual dimension and to prepare them for the gospel. We can build on such experiences, for sometimes people have encountered God but in an unfocused way. 'Yes', we may say, 'I think you've touched on the reality that there is a God, someone who's bigger and beyond you.'

Without any awkward crashing of evangelistic gears, you've travelled from vague experience to solid explanation of the truth of Jesus.

Telling Stories

AIM *To help a group identify the increasingly important role of story in communication today, and to look at how we may use stories to communicate the good news about Jesus.*

PART 1 Introduce the power of stories by asking the participants to reflect on the use of stories in TV soaps. Arrange a little competition. Split the group into pairs and give each pair a pen and piece of paper. Give them a minute to list as many soap operas as they can think of, and to identify with a star which they watch! Then compile a complete list on a large piece of paper with boxes opposite the names to indicate how many people watch each one.

☐ What do people enjoy about the most popular soap opera?

☐ Why are soap operas watched by so many people?

☐ Why have the soap operas that are based around more normal scenarios stood the test of time, while more extravagant ones have been dropped?

Photocopy the work sheet opposite on to an OHP or write up the questions on a piece of paper. Use the questions to summarize the group's findings and to consider how telling our own stories of faith can be important in evangelism.

PART 2 Photocopy the guidelines on pages 28-9 and ask everyone to read them. Then allow everyone 15-20 minutes to write out their story using the outline of their choice.

If you have time, ask one or two people to tell their stories and ask the rest of the group to listen as interested non-Christians. What bits were interesting? What words or phrases would mean little? What things need further explanation?

PART 3 If time, you could end the session by choosing a contemporary issue and seeing if the group can identify what is at the heart of that issue. Is there a Bible story which would throw some light on the issue and the way we should approach it? How might a Christian use this story in conversation with others to help bring a Christian perspective to bear?

Telling Stories

In many areas of life today, stories are used to communicate important realities. A 'story' does not mean a fairy story or a child's bedtime story, but an account of something that has happened — a newspaper story. In our changing culture, as explanation gives way to experience as the basis of knowledge, the use of story is likely to be a dominant theme in communication. There are many cultures in the world, including the culture of Jesus' day, where story is the primary means of communicating knowledge.

What are the different types of story?

Why are stories so helpful?

What are the stories we have to tell as Christians?

How can these stories be used to help us to tell others about Jesus?

Are stories the answer, or do we need more than stories?

CPAS © 1994

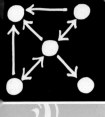

Jesus and Paul: Two Bible Studies

Read Luke 7:36-50

☐ In a single phrase, what teaching does Jesus want to convey?

☐ What does Jesus 'say' about God by allowing the woman to wash and anoint his feet?

☐ What is the point of Jesus' story about two debtors? What effect do you think there would have been if Jesus had immediately told Simon what he thought without first relating the story?

☐ Why is the story so powerful?

Read Luke 8:1-15

☐ What is so surprising about verse 10? Why did Jesus tell parables?

☐ If the church is the farmer, scattering the word of God, what response should we expect from our evangelism?

☐ Why do you think many people today remember the parable of the sower?

Read Acts 13:16-52; 17:16-34; 19:1-41; 28:17-31.

The passages all describe how Paul preached to, and talked with, unbelievers.

☐ When Paul wanted to communicate with an audience that was not necessarily on his side, what methods did he use?

☐ How effective do you feel Paul's methods were?

☐ From these passages, what guidelines can we find for our own evangelism?

Communities of Hope

If our friends and neighbours are going to believe in Christ, they need to see Christianity lived. There are reasonable arguments in support of the Christian faith, but our culture does not 'listen to reason'. However, it *is* looking for a way to live together, to sustain relationships in families and communities. There is no stronger evidence for the truth of the gospel than a community of people who believe and live it — people who show by their love that Christianity is not just another personal preference for those who like that sort of thing, but a lifestyle and world view that works because it is true.

Community matters

Exposure to the life and relationships of the local church is an important stage in evangelism. Let new people see what they are letting themselves in for!

___

66 The life and morale of the church is particularly important, because if morale is low among church members they will not ask their neighbours to come to church. "Come and be bored with me" is not inviting. 99
John Finney *Finding Faith Today*

___

All this cuts both ways. If 'not-yet Christians' need to see Christian community to be convinced, we need it to maintain our witness. The values of Jesus are so different to much of today's culture that we can not maintain them on our own. I'm not talking

about a 'gas-ring' community: 'all turned inwards and burning brightly'! This is the sort of church where newcomers are either not noticed or told to move because 'I always sit there'. The distinctive thing about Christian community is that it is about serving others. There is no point witnessing about Christ if our churches are not hospitable to newcomers.

___

66 Christian community is not primarily about togetherness. Togetherness happens, but only as a by-product of the main project, being faithful to Jesus. 99
Hauerwas and Wilimon *Resident Aliens*

___

Love and hospitality are distinguishing marks of genuine Christianity; so also is worship. Worship is the Church's most distinctive activity; it is also a vital resource for service and witness in the community. Although Christians are only a small proportion of the population, recent surveys of values show that a much larger proportion of those who work sacrificially in their local community are also regular worshippers. To maintain a lifestyle of sacrifice it seems it is necessary to give yourself regularly in love and surrender to the one who made and forgave us. When we worship we refocus our vision of our God and find new strength to serve others in his name.

Without worship we shrivel and become self absorbed and crabby. With worship there is an opportunity for a new reality of community and an encounter with God that transforms our lifestyle. For a society that's skeptical about any truth claims, this has to be a powerful evidence of the claims of Christ.

Another kind of pluralism

In our pick 'n'mix pluralist culture, the Church must not, dare not, be pluralist about truth. It is vital that we hold on to the uniqueness of Jesus and his claims.

I believe it is possible to do that without disparaging the beliefs of our neighbours. As far as truth is concerned, our response to pluralism is always going to be *no*.

But there's another kind of pluralism – and I think we're going to have to be increasingly open to it. This pluralism is based around, 'It ain't *what* you say, it's the *way* that you say it....'

As well as being plural in its beliefs, our society is becoming increasingly plural in its *forms* – its ways of doing things. It's a distinction made in an earlier chapter.

Within our society there's a dizzying diversity of ways of dressing, behaving, speaking and expressing individuality. Every age group, income group and social group produces its own particular sub-cultures. Some are long lasting, others as fleeting as fashion.

And if we're honest with ourselves, this is something we can see in our churches. We may claim the one Sunday service suits all people. But that's what John Finney, when he was the Officer for the Decade of Evangelism, called the 'Anglican Myth'.

One gospel — many clothes

A variety of forms of worship needn't necessarily be unhealthy. There's only one gospel, but in our diverse society we need to be able to offer that central truth in as many ways as possible. What we need is one gospel, yet many different clothes to dress it in.

I recommend that churches with more than one Sunday service unashamedly develop a different style and character for each one, targeting them at different sections of the local community. That way more people can be reached than by having services that are intended to be accessible for everyone but never can be. All churches should consider church planting to reach new groups. But some simply need to start a new service at a different time.

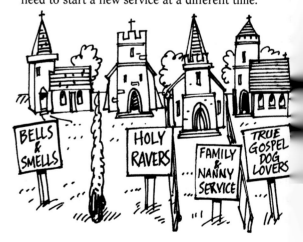

'..... *targeted at different sections of the local community.*'

I also suggest that churches in the same neighbourhood should not be threatened by one another or compete with one another. Rather, they

should develop a local strategy where each can work to their strengths (perhaps with tough teenagers or mums and toddlers) rather than have everyone trying to reach everyone without any coordination and without enough resources.

Working in partnership

I can hear the objection. Doesn't this development of different styles emphasize one of the most unattractive features of our congregations? Doesn't it highlight our divisions and play to the worst feature of our consumer culture, that we will only choose what we find comfortable?

It could do, but it need not.

The gospel breaks down social barriers, so every congregation that worships together regularly should have people in it who would not be together if it was not for Jesus. This means that some of our existing, rather monochrome congregations are a real obstacle to the gospel. But it does not mean that all Sunday services should feel the same. Unity allows diversity! It is possible to have varied congregations but each one represents the reconciliation Jesus brings, each has a distinctive character, and each is targeted for mission because the congregation is united in its commitment to win as many as possible for Christ.

And when it comes to working in partnership with other churches, what is godly about acting as

though either they do not exist or they are a threat? This sort of mutual competition is a direct cause of numerical decline. We need partnership.

What is our motivation for pursuing a rich plurality of form (not content) in outreach and worship? Our God is a God of rich diversity: with our eyes fixed on him there's nothing wrong with celebrating the rich plurality of our culture – in order to reach that culture.

What we are saying never changes. The *way* that we say it can and must change.

Serving in the new century

We have seen that we are living at a time of transition. A culture is dying. The agenda for its successor isn't fixed.

For a Decade of Evangelism the timing could hardly be better, or more challenging. Here in the West the cultural patterns for the new century are being set. What better time to think, pray and work through the meaning of mission?

We are all called to be involved: in our neighbourhood, in our area, in our town. I think that's a tremendously exciting privilege.

Services for All Seasons

AIM   *To discuss whether church services meet the needs of people in the community, and to consider where changes might be made.*

EXERCISE   Give a photocopy of the page opposite to each group member. Ask each to list the services that take place in their church throughout the week, including midweek communions and prayer meetings. Next, ask them to consider the brief character portraits and try to draw lines linking each person with a service.

☐ Where is it difficult, or even impossible, to draw connecting lines?

☐ Are there people with whom the group are in contact who don't find church services relevant or approachable? If there are, how might:

  – the local church change its services or add additional 'specialist' ones to cater for those uncomfortable with the present services?

  – the local church join with other local churches – or look to a neighbouring church – to provide something relevant? For example, should churches group together for youth work and youth services?

  – the local church arrange events in more 'neutral' territory rather than in the church building?

☐ Is the current movement towards special services for different groups a good or even biblical route? Or should we uphold, at all costs, the belief that each service should reflect the whole of the church: young, old, single, married, employed, unemployed...?

Services for All Seasons

Church service/event	Day/time

Mary, a Christian since childhood. Now 50 and committed to the local church. Her husband George is not a believer but occasionally comes to church.

Janet, a single parent coping with Mark (3) and Jennifer (6 months). Her partner Paul walked out on her when Jennifer was known to be suffering from cerebral palsy.

Martin and Sally, career-minded business people running their own hairdressing salon in the town. Increasingly affluent; no children; few Christian sympathies.

Penny, teenage daughter of regular church goers. Now 15 and anxious to be independent. Finds regular church services boring.

Jack and Ruth, retired couple. Both ex-teachers but new to church going. Familiar with traditional church services but are not communicants as they are still uncertain of their faith.

Michael and Raymond, two homosexual men who have been living together for many years. Both have local office jobs and are concerned to help people in the community.

Brian, 20 years old and a sales assistant at a local store. Not a Christian, but sympathetic. His girlfriend Mandy is a regular church-goer. Very keen on sport and part of a Sunday-morning football team.

Helen, Jack and their mentally handicapped son Tom. Helen and Jack have a strong Christian faith. Tom can be disruptive and very difficult to handle.

Jane, a young mother and part-time GP. Finds the church anti-women and the language sexist. Feels undervalued by the church.

Sarah, a bubbly 7 year-old who was introduced to the church by a children's holiday club. Neither of her parents want to come to church.

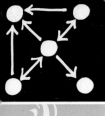

The Art of Communication

AIM *To encourage participants to think about and recognize the elements within a newspaper which help it to communicate and to use this as a way-in to discuss the different forms of communication in church services.*

PART 1 The person running the session should arrange, in advance, to have copies of tabloid and 'quality' newspapers. Split up into groups, with two newspapers per group. Choose one main story and ask the groups to highlight how that story is communicated in the different papers.

☐ How does the text capture the reader's interest?

☐ What use is made of personal stories?

☐ Which newspaper's print is the easiest to read?

☐ Do the headlines make you want to read the story? Which newspaper's headlines appeal most?

☐ Which newspaper contains most pictures? Do the pictures reduce the amount of news?

☐ Which newspaper contains the least number of pictures? Does it contain more news as a result?

☐ Are any pictures included for purely sensational reasons?

☐ Which pictures make you want to read the story?

Note: don't spend all the available time on this part of the exercise. Part 2 should not be squeezed out as it focuses on how communication works — or doesn't — within our church services.

PART 2 Newspapers communicate by combining gripping stories with eye-catching headlines, pictures and print. But what forms good communication within a church service? Is it the hymns, the sermon, or what?

Divide into small groups and ask these groups to list the elements in church services which combine to communicate God's message to us. (Church services are also about us serving God, but omit this dimension for this exercise.)

☐ Which elements help the communication, which hinder?

☐ Just as newspaper styles differ, which forms of service are relevant for those in the local community who seldom come to church?

☐ What should be changed to make the communication more effective?

☐ Should our Sunday services be tailored to specific groups of people just as a newsagent sells different newspapers?

40